For All Our Daughters

How Mentoring Helps Young Women and Girls Master the Art of Growing Up

For All Our Daughters

How Mentoring Helps Young Women and Girls Master the Art of Growing Up

Pegine Echevarria, MSW

For All Our Daughters: How Mentoring Helps Young Women and Girls
Master the Art of Growing Up

ISBN 1-886284-13-X
Library of Congress Catalog Card Number 97-77504
First Edition
ABCDEFGHIJK

Published by
Chandler House Press
335 Chandler Street
Worcester, MA 01602
USA

President
Lawrence J. Abramoff

Publisher/Editor-in-Chief
Richard J. Staron

Vice President of Sales, Publishing and Distribution
Irene S. Bergman

Editorial/Production Manager
Jennifer J. Goguen

Book Design
Bookmakers

Cover Design
Marshall Henrichs

Chandler House Press books are available at special discounts for bulk purchases.
For more information about how to arrange such purchases, please contact Irene
Bergman at Chandler House Press, 335 Chandler Street, Worcester, MA 01602, or
call (800) 642-6657, or fax (508) 756-9425, or find us on the World Wide Web at
www.tatnuck.com.

Chandler House Press books are distributed to the trade by
National Book Network, Inc.
4720 Boston Way
Lanham, MD 20706
(800) 462-6420

This book is dedicated to Mom, Aunt Lu, and Grandma.
Thank you! (*¡Muchísimas Graciás!*)

To all of the mothers, fathers, and mentors who strive to
make a difference in a girl's life.

Especially to David, my husband,
and to Brandon, my soul brother.

In memory of Allyson Pamela Henry

Contents

Foreword

❦

For All Our Daughters: How Mentoring Helps Young Women and Girls Master the Art of Growing Up inspired me to reflect on my life choices, my mentors of the past, and the mentors of today who continue to help me grow and learn.

After reading *Reviving Ophelia: Saving the Selves of Adolescent Girls* by Dr. Mary Pipher, I was taken aback by the pain and suffering that a growing number of girls today face. I was inspired to make a difference. My passion became *blue jean magazine* ®, the only magazine written and produced by young women from around the world. The teen editorial board is comprised of seventeen young women. Every Sunday we meet for teen board meetings where I have an opportunity to listen and learn from these dynamic young women. I have shared my experiences while feeling their pain, listening to their thoughts, and celebrating their excitement. During board meetings and in one-on-one conversations, they often share problems that they haven't shared with their parent(s). I realize that they trust me. How can I help them? What are the best ways to advise them? What can I teach them?

Pegine Echevarria, who serves on the advisory board and the board of directors of *blue jean magazine* ®, has advised me on how to mentor these young women. Pegine has been, and continues to be, an invaluable source of knowledge, support, and guidance. She openly shares her insights and advice. She has taught me that asking for help and learning to accept it is crucial to becoming a successful mentor and leader.

For All Our Daughters continues her legacy. By detailing her personal experiences mentoring girls and women, Pegine develops a new step in making a difference in girls' lives. She acknowledges that before we can learn how to help girls and ourselves master the art of growing up, we must first learn about the underlying issues and problems.

Sherry Handel
Publisher, Editor-in-Chief
blue jean magazine ®

Acknowledgments

The people I've been working with and the people who have been supporting this project have been invaluable to me. Their inspiration, advice, hard work, and dedication have made this book possible.

Thank you, David, my husband and partner, for reading the manuscript and offering your opinions; you made me laugh and love me unconditionally. Kenneth and Andrea, you have taught me so much about life, love, and laughter. Ida Echevarria, I can't tell you how much I value all of the lessons you have taught me and the stories you have shared—thanks, Mom. Aunt Lu, I don't know if you realize the impact you have had on my life; I hope that this book let's you know how much I love you and thank you. Grandma, *grácias*. Steven and Patti Gustafson, thank you for asking questions about reaching out to girls. You have taken the lessons in this book and implemented them with the girls in your neighborhood—thank you. Larry Schwartz, you are my Dad.

Brandon Toropov, from the moment we met we knew that we were on the same page. Thank you for your editorial work, input, guidance, questions, and creativity. Dick Staron, my publisher, you were there from the beginning; you taught me so much and your support has been invaluable. Irene Bergman, your support and strong feelings about girls has been a real source of strength. Larry Abramoff, thank you for your commitment to this project. Jennifer Goguen, your thoughts and editorial prowess are greatly appreciated. Carol Fass and Laura Donne, thank you for your enthusiasm, for your commitment to mentoring girls, and for making sure the world gets the message. I also want to thank Judith Burrows and Mary Toropov for your insights and support.

Many thanks are in order for Allie Casey and Ann Marie Ver Pault. Scout, your laughter, honesty, and strength have been inspirational and needed—thank you. Ann Marie, when I need a hug or a quick kick in the butt I know where to go—thanks, friend. Sherry Handel, publisher of *blue jean magazine* ®, our acquaintance was built on our commitment to girls; our friendship has been built on our trials and tribulations as business owners, our experiences with teens who have "been there, done that," and as women who have made a difference in each other's lives. Dominique Roniger, Loes Hekkins, and Sally Budde—the years have kept us going; thank you for your support. Amy and Rachel Gaddes, your relationship as mother and daughter, along with your insights, have been very helpful. Leeza Margolis, thanks for your words and your smile. Marty Margolis, you're not with us now, but our late night discussions proved inspirational.

My Girl Scout Troop 2476 in Nassau County, NY, thank you for letting me have fun. My Co-Leaders Nancy Rickman and Arleen Keene, thanks for your hard work, support, and understanding. Nancy, thank you for your help in my office.

I have had tremendous mentors who have given of themselves unconditionally. They have taught me so much and have seen in me more than I saw in myself. Anne Lown, social work was never the same after I met you. The hours you spent questioning me and provoking me have never been forgotten. Dottie Walters, author of *Speak and Grow Rich*, you opened my eyes to a whole new world and became a source of information as well as my cheerleader and teacher—thank you. Mark Victor and Patty Hansen, thank you for your hugs, your words, your enthusiasm, and your belief in me. Jack Canfield, thank you for your advice and support. Mark, Patty, and Jack, your book *The Aladdin Factor* taught me how to ask for what I want: I wanted to make a difference in the lives of women, girls, and Hispanics; you showed me how, thank you.

And lastly, I'm grateful to God for giving me the courage and conviction to go after my dream.

1

Why Girls Need More than Parents Can Give

*I'm not worried about her. We have a great relationship.
My daughter tells me everything.*

I hear words like these from many of the mothers I meet during my seminars. The truth is, your relationship with your daughter may be great, but that doesn't mean she will share everything of importance with you, and it certainly doesn't mean she's getting all the advice and guidance she needs as she approaches womanhood.

It's part of the maturing process for your daughter to stop turning to parents when faced with certain challenges. Girls—all girls—reach a point in their growth when they must construct individual identities by moving away from mothers and fathers. Helping your daughter learn to manage that momentous phase of her growth without exposing herself to pointless risk, exploitation, or abuse is one of the most difficult jobs any parent will ever face. This book offers a proven strategy that will, without any ifs, ands, or buts, help your girl to make it through to adulthood safe and sound—or minimize the long-term impact of past problems. I've seen the strategy work countless times. As a parent, you can count on the program that this book outlines—but you should be aware that there is a catch. It challenges you to accept that, as much as you might like to, you can't be everything for your daughter.

A Note to Parents (and Potential Mentors)

This book is meant for those who are willing and eager to take action to make a positive difference in the lives of girls and young women between the ages of nine and eighteen. If there's someone in your life who fits this description, and whom you care about, then you owe it to her to take advantage of the ideas and strategies that appear between these covers.

If you're not a parent, you'll want to learn how to use the ideas in this book to benefit a girl who needs your help. And if you are a parent with a daughter who falls in the age range I'm discussing, you probably already know that there's work for you to do—but you may not know that much of it is work you won't be able to do solely by relying on the strength of the bond you and your daughter now share.

Please don't misunderstand me. Your connection with your daughter may be wonderful. It may be full of moments of intimacy, caring, and genuine support and mutual respect. It may be as full of love and trust as any parent/child relationship can possibly be. But the sobering fact remains that you can't guide your daughter through this period on love alone. You need help.

The work you have to do is, for some parents, excruciatingly difficult. You have to bring someone else into your daughter's life, someone whom you trust implicitly, and who will know things about your daughter that you won't know.

There are a number of crisis points that will come up in your daughter's life as she manages the difficult transition from girlhood to young womanhood. If your daughter reaches her eighteenth birthday without having confronted at least one of the thirteen problems discussed later in this chapter, she'll be a statistical anomaly. And the truth is that you almost certainly won't be consulted about any of these momentous events.

That's because no parental relationship, in and of itself, is strong enough to see a daughter through these years.

For some parents, acknowledging this fact is difficult. But it must be acknowledged as a starting point, because the hurdles our daughters must clear are daunting ones.

Many of the parents I work with are surprised when they learn—or are reminded—of the serious emotional, physical, and developmental challenges that girls and young women face during the critical phase of youth and adolescence. These challenges are, I believe, very different than those faced by young boys. Not even the world's greatest parent can manage them exclusively within the confines of the immediate family.

At, say, nine or ten years of age, and continuing for several years, girls begin to focus powerfully on their need to be independent. Privacy becomes a concern (and sometimes an obsession), and the ability to pursue new and perhaps solitary activities becomes important. Your daughter may start making what seem to be extreme delineations between "her world" and "your world"—usually expressed as control of a defined space and specific possessions. All of this reflects an underlying desire to establish control in situations that may suddenly seem strange and unfamiliar to your girl. Powerful emotions are beginning to emerge in her life. After years of trying to find ways to please you, she now needs to find outlets for the expression of "negative" responses—without worrying about whether others will be pleased by her opinions and actions. Sometimes, her relations with family members (including you) will be very tense indeed.

At perhaps eleven years of age, your daughter reaps a whirlwind of change that will, for the next seven to ten years, affect her development on virtually every level: physical, cognitive, moral, emotional, social, and sexual. The development of an individual identity separate from that of one's parents takes on dramatic (and sometimes exasperating) new forms. Sexual maturity is a huge issue—your daughter begins to integrate the physical changes of puberty and comes to terms with the fact that her physical development, or lack thereof, is immediately apparent to others who interact with her.

As a general rule, girls begin to mature earlier than boys, and their sexual development is evident when breast formation begins. My experience is that girls also feel the many changes of puberty in a way very different from boys. Whether she likes it or not, whether she means to or not, whether it's fair or not, your daughter now makes a sexual statement every time she walks into a room that contains other people. Coming to terms with this reality can be an extremely difficult emotional and social process—especially when girls find themselves pigeonholed by males (young and old) who make assumptions about sexuality based on the prominence of a young woman's breasts or other evidence of physical development. Such pigeonholing often leads to intense pressure for girls to enter into situations they're simply not ready to handle.★

I think most women can remember a long-lasting period of profound confusion and frustration following the realization that one was no longer a little girl, and that one's body was perpetually "on display" and had a powerful impact on others. Girls are often unprepared for these changes—but the necessity that they develop identities separate from their role within the immediate family keeps them from reaching out to parents as they might have done a few years earlier.

★ It's worth noting in passing here that a startlingly large percentage of teen pregnancies are the result of relationships teenage girls enter into with adult men. Men often play the leading role in establishing these sexual liaisons with teenagers.

All the available evidence points to a period of extraordinary danger for girls and young women trying to master the art of growing up in today's world. A recent article in the *New York Times* reported that "Several studies ... have documented that more often than not, young girls entering puberty experience a crisis in confidence that renders them vulnerable to risky ... behaviors that they may not have the strength or will to resist." (*New York Times*, November 4, 1997, page C9.) The *Times* went on to report that nearly a third of girls surveyed reported suicidal thoughts—and that roughly four out of every ten girls in the fifth through twelfth grades reported "either smoking, drinking, or using drugs in the past month." Nearly a million teenage girls a year have to deal with the consequences of pregnancy—and in the vast majority of cases, of course, the pregnancy is unplanned.

The cascade of jaw-dropping statistics goes on and on. Even if your daughter is now unaffected by such problems, she certainly knows someone in her own age group who is grappling with daunting personal problems of one kind or another. How will she react? What choices will she make when her turn comes to confront these issues?

Difficult Decisions

The social environment within which every girl and young woman in our society must grow up is, unfortunately, not a particularly comforting one. It is a distinctly scary environment, with tough choices that carry difficult implications. Bear in mind that the world your daughter is entering is a good deal scarier for her than it is for you. Yet she must—

and she will—learn to make those choices outside of your sphere of influence.

These are difficult words for any parent of a young girl to read. Perhaps, as you read them to yourself just now, you made a silent vow to rededicate yourself to the job of raising your daughter well. to listen more, to offer more moral support, to point the way past hurdles with more compassion and intelligence.

That's a natural reaction. Even a parent who enjoys a superb relationship with a teenage daughter will wonder, "Am I doing enough?" In most cases, unfortunately, the honest answer is "No." Not because there's any lack of good intentions on your part, but because you alone can't guide your daughter through the rough waters she is now navigating. No parent can. You can provide information. You can offer insight and perspective. But you cannot do the job on your own.

External support from a nonparental female role model is an essential—and far too frequently ignored—requirement for healthy development in girls and young women. And it's hard to ignore the possibility that today's far-flung, media-saturated, divorce-damaged family structures have left more and more girls and young women adrift without such role models. Perhaps that's why so many of the terrifying statistics we read about self-confidence, academic performance, substance abuse, and sexual activity among young girls seem to have gotten worse in recent years. Fifty years ago, marriages were more stable than they are today, and families had more long-term female role models to supplement the work that mothers did. Today, connections with caring adult women are harder to come by.

You have to find a way to point your daughter toward such a trustworthy role model—whether she's an aunt, a cousin, a grandmother, a Girl Scout leader, a teacher, a friend from across the street, or some other caring, responsible woman—because your daughter's survival depends on it. If you want your daughter to emerge from the crisis years as a healthy, well-adjusted adult, you need to reach out to another woman. If such a role model isn't immediately available, you need to take the initiative and find someone who will step in and play that role.

Reaching out in this way doesn't represent a failure of parental technique. When it comes to girls and young women, failing to help your daughter connect with another adult woman is the real neglect.

Your Daughter Won't Share Everything with You

No matter how good your communication is with your daughter, no matter how well things seem to be going on the surface, there are things she will not and cannot tell you—things she needs desperately to tell someone. And that someone has to be an adult woman—a mentor—typically someone who makes a (subtle) first move to reach out to the girl. Establishing oneself as a mentor is an art that must be practiced, but it's not that difficult to learn. Once the connection is made, the difference a mentor can make in the life of a young girl can mean the difference between life and death.

I know, because I've benefited from these mentor relationships, and because I've served as mentor for countless young girls, some of them in very desperate straits indeed; and I've worked with countless families where the introduction of a nonparental female role model had a dramatic, sudden, positive effect in the life of a young girl at risk. There can be no replacement for this relationship. Girls and young women need another woman, another anchor point, if they are to develop and mature in a healthy way.

When a girl has a mentor, she begins to open up about important issues that are, for a variety of reasons, simply impossible for her to discuss with her mother (or her father, for that matter). As parents, we have complex emotional relationships with our daughters. Many of them are frightened of disappointing us or challenging our belief system. Often, it's hard for us to give advice that doesn't sound like a lecture. Lectures aren't what our daughters need or want, so certain topics simply never come up. The days when you can count on a "share all, tell all" approach with your daughter—say, around the ages of seven and eight—don't last long.

It's not that girls are being dishonest or trying somehow to live double lives. They want to discuss questions that matter to them. In fact, they're usually desperate to discuss these questions. But they need a "neutral party," someone they can trust who isn't Mom or Dad. The development of a close emotional relationship with a caring, trusted older woman who isn't a parent is an essential part of the maturation process. When that relationship doesn't exist, there are big problems.

Girls and young women today have enough problems to deal with already. Without further ado, take a look at my list— it outlines thirteen things girls are far more likely to share with a mentor than with a parent. If you believe that it's impossible for your daughter to encounter any of these problems during her own crisis years, you may be in for a rude awakening someday! These are the kinds of confidences I hear day in and day out from girls in all walks of life and all social groupings. The question is not whether or not one of these situations will apply to your daughter. The question is, will she have someone besides you to turn to when it's time to discuss them?

Thirteen Crises

If your daughter doesn't have to confront at least one of the crises reflected in the statements below by the time she's eighteen, she's in a tiny minority. When she does confront one or more of these problems, she's likely to try to talk to someone else before she talks to you. Make sure she's got access to someone who will listen and offer a mature perspective. Friends at the mall may mean well, after all, but they don't have the life experience necessary to offer all the support your daughter will need.

Help your daughter manage these thirteen potentially devastating events. Find a way to encourage her to connect with a responsible, caring woman who will help her make sense of a world that seems, too often, to offer little support and relevant insight. (You'll find specific ideas on how to reach out to mentors in Chapter Three of this book.)

1. **I had sex last night.** Studies indicate that 53.1% of all high school students have had sexual intercourse at some point; 14.45% have had sex with four or more sexual partners. More than half of all high school seniors have had sexual intercourse. We're all familiar with titillating talk shows' trumpet topics like "I Was a Teenage Sex Kitten." The truth is that the modern mass media is saturated with sex and sexuality. Despite even a firm grounding in strong morals and values, peer pressure and societal influences can be quite strong. A mentor can help your daughter make sense of "sales talk" she is likely to encounter from boys (i.e., "You would if you loved me,") and can help to counteract some of the most offensive media messages (such as fashion and perfume ads that exploit youthful sexuality).

2. **I had unprotected sex.** Do you think I have AIDS? Nearly half of currently sexually active high school students did not report using condoms during their last sexual intercourse. Boys claimed to have used condoms at a higher rate than girls, leaving open the possibility that a certain amount of exaggeration prevails. A trusted mentor can reinforce or supply important information about birth control and protection from sexually transmitted diseases—something you won't be able to do if your child decides, as many do, to take you "out of the loop."

3. **I'm pregnant.** Twenty-five percent of all first births in this country are to teen mothers between the ages of fifteen and nineteen. Girls talk to someone else first because they are afraid of what their parents, especially their mothers, will say and do. With a trusted, responsible mentor in your daughter's circle, you will have a "silent ally" who will almost certainly lobby to get you all the facts, and, at the very least, help to verify the pregnancy and point your child toward responsible medical care. Most important of all, your child will have someone who will listen openly.

4. **I've been smoking for a while; everyone at school does.** Smoking among teenage girls is again rising, despite massive efforts from government agencies and various media outlets to get the word out on the health dangers of tobacco. If a girl begins to smoke, the habit usually begins between the ages of ten and sixteen. Having a trusted mentor means having someone impartial to talk to about the pros and cons of smoking—in all likelihood, someone who can appeal effectively to natural concerns about appearance and smell, and thus help to change the behavior.

5. **I got drunk last night.** The percentage of eighth graders reporting daily use of alcohol rose by nearly half between 1995 and 1996. The percentage of eighth graders reporting having been drunk in the past month increased from 8.3% to 9.6% in the same period. Nearly a third of high school seniors reported

having been drunk in the past month. A mentor can help put questions about alcohol and drug abuse in the proper perspective—and can help out in the (common) circumstance of a close friend who has a serious drinking problem.

6. **I want to kill myself.** A staggering 29% of adolescent girls reported having thoughts of suicide. From 1980 to 1992, the rate of suicide among young white females increased 233%. In such situations, having a trusted adult to appeal to can literally mean the difference between life and death.

7. **I throw up after each meal.** Eating disorders are a particularly pronounced risk for girls, and they're likely to be connected in complex ways to a girl's relationship to her parents. This is another situation where an adult female friend can exercise a literally lifesaving influence. Such a mentor can help to reinforce basic self-esteem, and can also make it clear (often by personal example) that successful women come in all shapes and sizes

8. **My mom doesn't care about me; she's not interested.** (or: She won't give me any privacy.) Thirteen percent of girls surveyed reported having no one to turn to when stressed, overwhelmed, or depressed, or for information about health. Nearly half did not name their mother as the person to whom they would turn for emotional support. Girls who had depressive symptoms or who reported

abuse were far more likely than other girls to say they had no one to turn to. These girls were also less likely to report that they would turn to their mothers for support. Feelings of neglect or disinterest can have many causes. Conflicts with parents over issues of privacy and autonomy can be jarring for both sides and can leave you and your daughter feeling both betrayed and hopeless. Irresponsible behavior from your child may lead you to try to control or account for her actions; without a mature, nonparental role model for your child to talk to, this cycle of conflict can escalate into dangerous patterns indeed. With such a mentor, relationships stand a much better chance of maintaining some kind of balance.

9. **I hate myself.** Nearly one in every four girls surveyed exhibited depressive symptoms; one in ten showed "severe" depressive symptoms. Girls scored notably worse in this area than boys did. Many parents of girls with self-hatred and depression problems are profoundly shocked at the degree to which the issues have gone unnoticed and unexamined; a trusted adult mentor can help your daughter talk through issues of concern without having to maintain a habitual "everything's fine" image.

10. **I want the pill.** (or: I need to talk to a doctor.) The leading reason adolescents gave for not getting needed medical care or birth control consultation was reluctance to tell parents about a problem or situation. Two

out of every five girls cited this concern. A mentor can help your daughter fill in the areas where information is lacking and provide support for informed, responsible decisions.

11. **He hit me.** One study found "disturbingly high incidence of violence, with 18% of girls in grades five through twelve reporting some form of physical or sexual abuse." My own experience as a counselor is that parents are often kept in the dark about such relationships. If your daughter is involved in an abusive relationship with a man of any age, she's likelier to find a way to extricate herself from it if she has a trusted, mature woman to talk to about the problem. A mentor can offer empathy, guidance, and insight on dealing with men who have a need to abuse and control. This is another area where a mentor can have a significant positive impact on your daughter for years to come, and perhaps even save her life.

12. **(An older male friend or relative) keeps coming on to me/sending me love notes.** As a general rule, most abuse occurs at home, occurs more than once, and occurs as a result of the actions of a family member or friend of the family. Girls are often sworn to secrecy or physically threatened in an effort to maintain silence. They may have serious reactions of shame, guilt, and self-hatred following these episodes. It will be far easier for a girl to raise this issue with someone who is not a family member than with someone who is; a responsible mentor will almost certainly bring the problem to your attention immediately.

13. **This guy made me do something I didn't want to do.** Nearly one in ten older girls answered "yes" when asked whether "a boyfriend or date has ever forced sex against your will." When girls who reported date-forced sex were included with those who reported sexual or physical abuse, the total group represented one in four high school girls. When there is a trusted adult mentor to appeal to, your daughter will be much less likely to fall into a negative relationship spiral. She is also less likely to be psychologically or physically traumatized any further.

(Sources for the various statistics cited: Child Trends, Inc. Study, 1994; Youth Risk Behavior survey, Center for Disease Control and Prevention, 1995; and Commonwealth Fund survey of fifth through twelfth graders, 1997; National Institute on Drug Abuse reports; Carnegie Council on Adolescents report.)

What to Do?

The "big thirteen" above is only a partial list—other topics your daughter may need to discuss, but may be unwilling to discuss with you, include educational plans; friends you like but she doesn't; friends she likes but you don't; and body image issues. If your daughter does not have a trusted, mature woman to reach out to—if she doesn't have someone who will teach her how to handle challenges and build supportive relationships outside the family—she is needlessly courting catastrophe.

What can parents do within the home environment? Attempting (belatedly) to "lay down the law" about any of the issues raised above is usually a mistake, as is attempting to force your daughter to discuss matters she's unwilling to address. Here are some of the most important steps you can take in the home to help prevent the emergence of the kinds of crises we've been looking at. The earlier you put these principles into practice, the better off you and your daughter will be.

- Develop limitless reservoirs of patience.

- Support your daughter emotionally (even in the face of occasional ambivalence, hostility, or serious errors in judgment).

- Allow your daughter her own physical space and grant her a measure of control over it; respect her privacy.

- Frame rules in terms of what can be done ("You can stay out until 10:00 p.m.") instead of what can't ("I don't want you staying out late."). Most girls will respect their parents' limits—if parents respect theirs. At the same time, however, you should...

- Expect some form of rebellion against adult rules.

- Learn not to respond instinctively—try to listen to what she has to say.

- Allow some form of group hang-out for her and her friends.

- Permit independent social interaction within a safe environment—an environment that will allow your daughter to establish an identity that interacts with members of the opposite sex. (Any attempts to rule out contact with boys, or strictly control all aspects of that contact, are likely to backfire.)

As important as the principles outlined above are, I believe the most important step you can take is to bring a mature woman into the picture for your daughter—and to learn exactly what kind of role that woman should play in her life. Fortunately, that's what the rest of this book is all about. So read on!

2

One Girl's Story, One Mentor's Story

My decision to become a mentor, and to learn about child and adolescent development, was the result of some extraordinary events in my own life. I was lucky enough to have an ongoing series of supportive relationships with strong women who helped me to master the difficult art of growing up. I want to take some time now to give you some important background about what happened to me when I was growing up, how I benefited from the support of the mentors in my own life, and the early lessons I learned about reaching out to girls and young women. My story is not the "pattern" for the stories of the millions of girls who need help. Some of those girls face less intense challenges than I did, and some face problems that are much more severe, or even life-threatening. But they are all our daughters, and they all need guidance as they manage the journey that leads out of girlhood and into womanhood. My experience with seminar participants leads me to believe that learning about what happened to me may help you help your girl make some sense out of what's happened to her.

I was born in 1956 in a small town in upstate New York. My mom met my dad when she was working in Philadelphia as a buyer. She was twenty-six years old, a college graduate (the first ever in her family), and she appeared to have a bright future ahead of her. She had her sights on a career as an executive in the garment industry.

Then my mom and dad decided to get married, even though my grandfather was dead-set against the idea. This could have had something to do with my dad's history: He had been married before; and there were three kids from his first marriage.

After their wedding, my father made a pronouncement: "We are moving to New York, I have a new job." My mom had to give up the job she loved. My father worked as the manager in a restaurant for a while—eventually, the two of them moved to Newburgh, New York. His other kids would come around often; after I was born, they came to live in our house. My mom took care of all of us.

Despite my father's often-stated desire to be the sole breadwinner for the family, money got tight; to help make ends meet my mom worked as a waitress at a truck stop for a while. Her sister and our grandmother never visited our family. I think there must have been lingering resentment about the choices my dad had made and the price my mom had paid for some of those choices.

Leaving the Degree Behind

If there were misgivings on my mom's side of the family, they must have intensified with each new downturn in my dad's career. He lost several jobs in a row; eventually, we lost our house. We had to move in the middle of the night. It was apparently quite a frenetic operation, one driven by a good deal of pain and a short period of time in which to experience it. My mom was forced to leave in such a hurry that she didn't have time to take any of the family's most treasured heirlooms and honors. She literally had to leave her degree behind.

That was an awful night, a night that has never left my mother's memory. (And her frequent retellings of it have never left *my* memory.) In addition to having to leave behind her college degree, she also had to leave behind many of her own physical possessions—including anything of interest from her own childhood—and the vast majority of my baby clothes and mementos. My family only possesses a single picture of me as a baby.

The years that followed were difficult ones for my mom. We found ourselves living in a tiny apartment in the Bronx—a tough, racially diverse neighborhood. Our financial situation was so tight that any dreams my mom might have had of making her way into the garment industry seemed very far away indeed. And the fights between my mom and my dad kept getting worse and worse. Only now, as an adult, can I understand how difficult my mom's life must have been at that point. She was in a deteriorating relationship with a man her family had never taken to, and whose presence in her life had caused her to lose contact with many of the people she loved. She was living in a dingy apartment in the inner city. She had two young kids to take care of—me and my brother—which is, of course, a huge job in and of itself. And her family was always broke.

As luck—or fate—would have it, my mom became friendly with my kindergarten teacher, Mrs. Finkel. I've often thought to myself that my mom's relationship with this woman was one of the great blessings in our lives—because if she hadn't been able to learn about teaching from Mrs. Finkel, I never would have embarked on a career as counselor and mentor for young girls.

Mrs. Finkel encouraged my mom to study for a teacher's license and work with young children, and that's exactly what she did. I don't know how she pulled it off, given the tumult and financial pressure in our household around this time. My dad lost yet another job, we lost our tiny apartment, and the whole family moved in with my Aunt Lu. (Eventually, we decided to move in with my grandmother.) But in the middle of all the chaos, my mom pulled it off. She earned her teacher's license, and she started teaching. The same textbooks my mom studied became *my* primary reading material as I was growing up. I was as fascinated by the subjects of learning and child development as she was—a fact that had a huge impact on my adult career choices!

That meant more income for what was—at this point—a very large family that could use every penny that came its way. Although there were now three strong women in our

household—my grandmother, my aunt, and my mother—
times were still tumultuous. My half-sister had moved in,
having worn out her welcome with my dad's first wife. My
dad didn't put a great deal of attention into helping her out.
There were many fights over values—at age thirteen, my
half-sister was sexually active and had a habit of putting herself in situations that were dangerous, compromising, or
both. As a professional, I can look at the situation now and
realize how much pain she must have been in and imagine
the kinds of risks she was running in her life. At the time,
however, all that seemed to matter was that she was making
my mom furious.

There were epic fights about her (apparently equally
epic) "social life"—fights that my dad disengaged from, and
my mom waged dutifully. I realize now how hard it must be
for a step-parent to impose a value system, or any meaningful "limits" on an unhappy girl who doesn't feel like
listening to another litany about how many mistakes she's
making. But I know my mom did her best.

My half-sister started to run away from home. My mom
would walk through the streets, looking for her—and eventually find her—in some of the seediest places in town. This
happened five or six times. Finally, my mom told my half-
sister, "If you run away again, I'm not going after you."

She ran away again. My mom didn't go after her.

No one heard from her for several years, and she made
some big mistakes during that period. I could tell at the
time that the episode had bothered my mother a great deal.

It was only when I became a mother myself that I knew exactly why she had looked at me with such an odd, concerned, distracted expression in the weeks and months that followed my half-sister's departure.

My mother was worried—deeply worried—that I was about to follow in my half-sister's footsteps. And she had reason to be.

The Power Play

For one thing, my parents' marriage was now coming apart at the seams, which left me feeling a good deal of turmoil in my life. My mom had threatened to leave my dad several times—one spring, she decided to go one better and kick him out of the house. She told him she was going to Mexico for a divorce.

True to her word, she did just that, and she left my brother and me in the care of my grandmother. Not long after that, my father waited for a time when he knew my grandmother would be out of the house—and came and took us away. It was strange and disorienting, the way he managed it. I didn't know what the term kidnapping meant, but I realize now that that definitely described what happened to us. I didn't understand what was going on, why my father had taken us away from my grandmother. I wanted to go back to my mother, and I told him so in no uncertain terms.

When my mom heard what had happened from my grandmother (who was, as I found out later, close to hysterical), she called my father's house and told him that she was planning to arrive from Mexico on such and such a date and that we were to be in the front of our house when she arrived, and that if my brother and I weren't standing out front when she did, he'd pay dearly for it. When she pulled up, we were there.

But the matter wasn't settled. Later that evening, my father came back to our house and started banging on the front door and shouting at the top of his lungs. We tried to ignore it for a while. He kept on pounding and kept on screaming. The awful sounds got louder and louder. Finally, he broke the door down.

He stormed into the house and went after my mother. He started to beat her. He was swinging hard, and he was angrier than I'd ever seen him—not my father, but a demon who had taken over his body for some reason. My blood turned to ice.

People were yelling and screaming everywhere, but that didn't seem to stop him, or even slow him down. He kept swinging at my mother, then tried to grab my brother. I was pretty sure he wanted to take him away—split the two of us up. The thought that I might never see either my father or my brother again flashed through my mind. I felt physically ill.

My mother grabbed my brother by the arm and pulled at him, screaming that she wasn't going to let him out of the house. My aunt tried to get in the middle of the struggle, and my dad pushed her away. My brother was crying and yelling. What must have been going through his mind?

My aunt called the police. By the time they came, the house was something very close to a madhouse. I was standing on top of the bed and shouting "Shut up, shut up, shut up," over and over again. The police arrested my father and took him away—this at a time in our history when most cops were happy to simply separate the principals in "domestic problems" and leave everyone to "calm down." Not this time. They broke up the fight and led him away; they were very rough on him. I remember begging one of the officers not to hurt my daddy.

I was eight years old.

Promises and Betrayals

That night, I couldn't sleep, no matter how hard I tried. That image of my father beating my mother, striking her with all of his strength, wouldn't leave me. I remember thinking that things had gotten as bad as they could possibly get, that I'd gone through the worst troubles anyone could possibly have to experience. I was wrong.

After that awful night, we were supposed to see my father every weekend. That lasted for a while; then he started coming by every other weekend. Then one afternoon he returned from a trip with my brother, dropped the boys off, and, after hardly any time at all, promised he'd be back the following weekend to see me. I remember the smile on his face as he waved goodbye from behind the wheel.

That was the last time I ever saw him. I never understood how he could have abandoned me the way he did. I would call him, ask when I'd be able to see him, and hear him promise me that we'd get together "soon." But "soon" never came. Before long, he stopped returning our phone calls. My mother made call after call, trying to help me reconnect with him. Nothing worked. The man no longer wanted to be part of my life.

If I had a dollar for every time I stayed up late in my bed trying to figure out exactly what I'd done to make my father stop loving me, I'd be a very rich woman today. The only answer I ever came up with—that he was my father, and that he'd always been there for me before, and that whatever I'd done must have been something truly terrible—was only half an answer, one that made me feel low and dark and heavy inside.

I began to hate myself.

My mom worked hard to raise us right, and I think she did a great job. God knows being a single Hispanic mother in a tough neighborhood in New York was a challenging assignment for her. But bringing up a young girl was a job that she couldn't do alone. In fact, the premise of this book is that this is a job no one—or at least no parent—can do alone. There are struggles that girls go through that no parent can help girls understand or put in context—struggles that girls will not tell their mothers about, no matter how close the two of them are. Fortunately, when the time came, my mother was able to accept the importance of getting other women—strong women—into my life. If the years of struggle and difficulty I went through taught me anything, they taught me that a girl needs both the love of a parent and the support and guidance of a mentor to make sense of the trials that come her way during the years when she's forging her own womanhood. My mom was smart enough to realize that every daughter was one of "our daughters"—a daughter requiring the support, guidance, and encouragement of more than one adult woman. So she made the choice that probably saved my life. She made sure Aunt Lu played a part in my life. My mom sensed, at some level, that I wasn't going to be able to overcome the most critical struggles in life without someone besides her to reach out to.

Once my father vanished from the scene, my Aunt Lu took on a greater and greater significance in my life. She'd spend lots of time with me, bring me books, take me places, and—perhaps most important of all—always find an excuse to give me a hug and tell me that everything was going to be okay. She'd tell me that I came from strong stock, and that sometimes things happen in life that we have to try to make sense of as we go along. My Aunt Lu's message to me was, essentially, a religious message, even though it didn't have explicit religious content. She always tried to remind me that even though we don't always understand why things happen the way they happen, it doesn't mean that we're any less important or any less needed.

Aunt Lu always tried her level best to make me feel ready for the next struggle, big or little. She was a godsend. As it happened, the next big struggle came when I was twelve years old, and it very nearly sank me. I was on a country visit to my great-aunt's house—uncles, aunts, and cousins were everywhere. It was a lovely summer day, and the surroundings couldn't have been more beautiful, especially for a city girl: trees, grass, and gorgeous flowers were everywhere. The world was in bloom.

Day after day, the high point of the day would come when my cousins and I would play tag; we would race all over the hill, in between the trees. During one game, it was my turn to be "it." I ran up the hill, looking for someone's remote hiding place—far away, it turned out, from the group. And there, behind one of the trees, was my uncle. I'll call him Uncle Wally.

> "Peggy, come here." Wally was one of my favorite relatives, someone I really looked up to, a trusted friend.
> He said it again: "Peggy, come here."

Peggy is a name I've always hated—I'm not sure whether it's because of what happened that afternoon or because it simply doesn't fit my personality. I think I must have hated it before this incident took place. Don't ever walk up to me after a seminar and call me Peggy. You might not like what happens next.

> "Peggy," he said for the third time, "come here."
> "I can't," I answered. "I'm playing tag."

He didn't move; instead, he stood there and stared at me. I wasn't frightened. I was just eager to get back to the game and try to find where my cousins were hiding. But something in the way he looked at me told me he wanted me to come over to where he was. I decided to walk over to explain why I couldn't stop the game. When I got within an arm's length of him, he grabbed the back of my neck and held me firmly.

He pulled my face to his. Everything started spinning. I tried to move away, but he pulled me back. I remember thinking, in that instant, that I was like an animal—a rabbit or a mouse, say—that some hungry, larger animal might swoop down on. I remember feeling captured and thinking that I was about to be devoured. He pushed me down on the ground. I felt his heat on my face. His breath stank. I won't call what he was doing to my face "kissing," because I know what it's like to kiss someone, and this was a very different experience. His skin was rough and his stubble scratched my lips. When he put his tongue in my mouth, things started spinning even faster, and I almost threw up. (In retrospect, I wish I had vomited on him, but as it turned out, I spared him that indignity.)

He told me to be quiet. I don't think I could have talked if I'd wanted to. He pulled me closer—no asking, no instructions, just pulled my hips to him as though I were a rag doll, as though he owned me. "This," I remember thinking to myself, "is what it's like to be a thing."

All this time I'd thought I was a person. A bad person, of course—the kind of person who does something mystifyingly evil and causes her father to break off all contact without any explanation—but a person, nonetheless. Now, it turned out, I was a thing.

His pants were still up, but that hardly seemed to matter. I felt him pushing against me with a strange, insistent rhythm that he seemed to understand, but that was utterly new to me and quite terrifying. He wanted to possess me, every inch of me, and I realized that if I didn't find some way to stop him, he'd take over a part of me that I wouldn't be able to get back. I felt as though I'd been pulled into another dimension, as though I'd been betrayed (as in fact I had been) by one of my very closest friends.

It seemed I was suffocating. (I think I must have been holding my breath the whole time.) He seemed to have no idea how repulsive what he was doing felt to me. Actually, it was even worse: He didn't care what I thought about what he was doing to me. I was overpowered, a bauble he had every right to do with as he pleased. He would no more consult me about how I felt about all this than he'd ask a washcloth or a book or a piece of toilet paper for permission to do as he pleased.

I thought I'd hit bottom when my dad started attacking my mom, or when it became clear that my father had abandoned me and wouldn't make any effort to see me ever again. That was trouble. But this, I realized, was a new kind of trouble. This was trouble that scared you down deep to the marrow of your bones. This was trouble that changed who you were, changed how you thought of yourself, changed everything. This was big trouble, trouble that was going to get a whole lot worse if it didn't stop immediately.

He was clutching the small of my back. He kept thrusting and rubbing, making sounds I didn't want to think about then and don't want to think about now. I wish I could remember coming up with some final conclusion: "Hey, I've got an idea," or "He deserves something really awful," or even "I've had enough of this behavior from him." The truth is, though, that I wasn't thinking much of anything at that point. I was operating on survival instincts and one of them brought to the attention of my conscious mind the fact that my knee was positioned just about perfectly to deliver a powerful blow to my uncle's groin. While he was writhing and shifting and rubbing, that's just what I did. I kneed him for all I was worth.

It worked. He doubled over in pain. I stood up and ran.

I didn't tell anyone, not for a long, long time. He was a popular member of the family, a grownup, someone everyone respected. My self-esteem had been low enough going into this experience that it was relatively easy to talk myself out of trying to make any kind of stand about what he'd done to me. Who was I? No one would pay attention to what I had to say. I don't even think I got as far as wondering whether anyone—either in my family or out of it— would believe me. I just didn't want to have to think about it. I wanted it to be over for good.

But it wasn't over for good. After that, my sense of self started to drift away into some far region. I started to withdraw, to keep to myself, to feel worthless, like an outsider, like someone nobody wanted to have anything to do with—family, schoolmates, counselors, teachers, it didn't matter. I felt dirty, as though there were no me at the center of things anymore.

Withdrawal

The assault in the woods had heightened my (already powerful) feelings of inadequacy. By the time I was in the eleventh grade, I was completely withdrawn and terrified of social encounters at my school. This was not entirely unjustifiable, given the dangerous behavior of some of the crowds that circulated there, and the haughty attitude most of the other kids adopted toward me. I felt utterly isolated. I felt that, despite the best efforts of my mom and my Aunt Lu, if there were a set of rules to living life, somebody had forgotten to pass along a copy to me.

Once, several years after the fact, my mom and I had a conversation about the problems I was having dealing with other people, and I worked up the courage to tell her what had happened in the woods. She was furious—but, since so much time had passed, she decided not to try to take any legal action against my uncle.

I later learned that this uncle had tried the same thing on one of my father's daughters from his first marriage. He'd found my uncle on top of her, pulled out a gun, and put it to my uncle's head, warning him that if he ever tried anything like that again, he'd be a dead man.

Suppose, I thought to myself, that my father had stuck around, stayed on the scene. Suppose he hadn't cut himself out of my life entirely. Maybe he would have had some kind of influence on this man. Maybe my uncle would have been afraid to assault me. Maybe the whole thing would have turned out differently.

Somehow, learning that my dad had cared enough to stand up for one of his daughters—but had not cared enough to stand up for me, or at any rate not been around when I'd needed him to stand up for me—made everything worse. That hollow feeling deepened inside me.

A feeling of being somewhere else, somewhere other than where my body was, began to grow stronger and stronger in my life. It was as though I were habitually falling through space. There was a person named Pegine, but the animating force that was at the center of that identity was always in danger of drifting, dissolving, passing into a fine mist. I needed lessons, not just in the art of growing up, but in the art of being present.

Months passed without my sharing a single word of meaningful conversation with anyone. If someone had thought to diagnose me, I think I might have ended up in a mental hospital. Fortunately, that's not where I ended up. I ended up in the Junior Girl Scouts.

A New World

My scout leader, Mrs. Brantwell, gave me a sense of purpose, a sense of direction, a sense of belonging. It was exactly what I needed. Like so many of the women who do good mentoring work without knowing it (including my Aunt Lu), she had an intuitive grasp of what I needed. The five essentials you'll be reading about later in this book—physical development, intellectual development, emotional development, spiritual growth, financial accountability—all of those essentials exist in any number of healthy mentor relationships in which an older woman reaches out to a younger woman without ever having heard of a program like mine. In other words, some women are great mentors before they receive any formal training whatsoever. I believe Mrs. Brantwell was one of those women.

Mrs. Brantwell, who knew about my father's vanishing act, took a special interest in me—and, while she was one of the most supportive people I ever met, she also made a habit of challenging me. She challenged me to learn more about the world I lived in, challenged me to learn more about history and politics, challenged me to be a leader, challenged me to develop myself physically. It was through the Girl Scouts that I became close to Denise, a fellow scout whose father had passed away. I think Mrs. Brantwell realized that Denise and I were kindred spirits—she seems to have gone out of her way to make sure we both felt wanted and cared for. Most important of all, she listened to us—and she let us blow off steam. As you'll learn in later chapters of this book, that may be the most important mentoring skill of all. Mrs. Brantwell made Denise and me feel special, in much the same way that my Aunt Lu had made me feel special when I was so much younger. I believe she must have made a promise to herself not to lose either of us, and every day I thank God that she found a way to keep it—by listening to us, by helping us master scouting challenges, by taking us on trips, and by looking the other way when our unique brand of adolescent humor would have driven some other, less committed adult over the edge.

Mrs. Brantwell was there for me, and I honestly believe she kept me from falling apart during my teenage years. I wish I knew where she was now so I could thank her personally, but I don't. The only appropriate thanks I've been able to muster is to serve, today, as the leader of my own Girl Scout group. Perhaps that's enough.

Long Term, Short Term

Some mentor relationships endure for a few months; others last for years and years. My relationship with my Aunt Lu, thankfully, fell into the latter category. I can remember one New Year's Eve when she called me downstairs for a private talk; she was getting ready to go out for a New Year's Eve party. For some reason, she pulled me into the bathroom and started telling me how much she loved me and how proud she was of me for having made it through as far as I had. She kept telling me how strong I was, and how, even though I wasn't aware of the talents and the strengths that I had, that I was capable of achieving anything I wanted in my life. At the end of her talk, she gave me a beautiful diamond ring with three little diamonds. It had been given to her while she was in Cuba. I remember thinking how much she loved me as she put that ring on my finger. I can't tell you how many times over the years I've touched that ring when I was scared—and felt better as a result.

That talk with my Aunt Lu was one of the high points of my youth, a time when I was able to convince myself that I really was going to make it. My academic performance improved after that talk, and so did my ability to interact socially with others. It was a remarkable moment, because I had proof that somebody—not just my mom, but somebody different—went out of her way for me, did something undeniably special for me, showed how strong her faith in me was.

Aunt Lu was convinced I was strong enough to make it now. She was convinced I had what it took to be the best person I could possibly be, despite my dad's leaving, despite the assault I'd undergone, despite the drugs and gangs that surrounded us in the neighborhood where we lived. She was convinced I was worth something. And you know what? She was right.

An Ongoing Process

There are other women who made a big difference in my life—including a number of teachers who took the time to reach out to me—but I think you get the idea. I survived the bad neighborhood, and the family problems, and the sexual abuse, because someone reached out to me, and showed me, among other things, how to use the help other people had to offer—and how to demand the best from myself. And now I make it my business to reach out to girls and show them how to manage the same hurdles I overcame.

Effective mentoring is really the act of helping parents as they teach their girls how to form adult relationships and build adult support systems. That may sound straightforward enough, but it demands constant work in the five key areas you'll be reading about later in this book.

Consider the common problem of emotional with-drawal, for instance. I can remember a night when I was still in my "don't talk to me phase." My Aunt Lu and my mom had cornered me and said, in essence, "Look, you're going to a party with us, and you're going to reach out to some new people. Here's how you do it. First of all, remember that everybody is just as nervous about meeting new people as you are. So here's what you do: Make believe you're interested in them, make believe you already have a relationship with that person. Put your hand out and say, 'Hi! My name is Pegine. So tell me, what you brings you here and how do you know so-and-so?'"

Talk about a challenge! They dutifully brought me to this party and reminded me at every opportunity about what I was going to have to do. When the time came to actually talk to other people, I said, "I can't just do that." And my mom said, "Watch us."

And there they were, doing it. My mom walked up to a total stranger and said, "Hi. My name is Ida. How are you?" and shook the person's hand. In the other corner of the room, my Aunt Lu was doing the same thing.

That was a double-barreled lesson in adulthood—and a perfect example of how a parent and a mentor can work together to change a girl's life. The networking lesson I learned that night has had an immense impact on my life, my career, and my self-image. I honestly don't think I could have learned it from my mother alone.

It had taken a mentor. It had taken my Aunt Lu, working hand in hand with my mother. But it had happened. I was on my way.

Putting It into Practice

Some years later, I found myself following in my mother's footsteps—working with kids—and feeling more certainty

about my career choice than I'd felt about just about anything else in my life in a long, long time. I started out in this
field as a counselor to kids whose families were homeless.
Let me assure you that right now, today, kids can and do
face challenges that would decimate any number of adults.
To be young and homeless in New York City is a fate I
wouldn't wish on anyone.

One girl—a girl I feel certain was being sexually abused—
will always stay in my memory. I'll call her Kim. She was very
smart, although her reading and math skills were far below
what she would have needed to keep up in a public-school
environment. Kim was street-smart, though. She was wise
beyond her years, and also cynical beyond her years. I could
tell she had seen and experienced a great deal for a thirteen-
year-old, probably more than a thirteen-year-old should. I
tried desperately to work with her to find something she
could take pride in, something she could use as an anchor in
her life. I settled on theater and arts activities—because it
seemed like a much more likely pathway to building up her
self-esteem given the time constraints I was working under.
It seemed unrealistic for me to expect to bring her math or
reading skills up to par. After all, I only got to meet with her
once a week. Although her parents were clearly in the midst
of some serious drug and alcohol abuse problems, at least
they were enough on the ball to show up at the center where
I worked and let me meet with their daughter.

I tried hard to help Kim find a way to connect with some
activity that she could use to define herself in some positive
context. And I succeeded in attaining that goal—I got her

to open up and engage in the arts and theater activities I'd set up for her. I got her to take pride in herself. And, in so doing, I let her down so badly that I thought seriously about leaving my work with high-risk kids.

That may seem like a strange thing to say, but it's absolutely true. I was making a classic mistake of early entrants to the field (and, I might add, much of the bureaucracy set up to help troubled kids). I was focusing on curriculum, rather than on the needs of the girl. In other words, I was making choices based on the experiences I wanted Kim to have and the skills I wanted her to develop. I was doing so for a good reason—I suspected, rightly, that her self-esteem might rise if she took on some theater activities. But I left her relationship with me out of the equation, and in so doing, I made sure that she would descend once again.

Let me explain what I mean. Kim and I had a great experience together. She took part in theater activities and arts work, and she started to feel as though the world might just make sense. But it took my physical presence for her to feel that way, and I knew—or at least should have known—that, given Kim's circumstances and the realities of the lifestyle her parents led, I wasn't going to be a permanent part of this girl's life. Even if I had somehow been able to take on a long-term role with her, all the theater and arts work in the world, in and of itself, wasn't going to give her what she needed. Kim needed to learn how to build her own support networks. She needed to be able to find out how to reach out to other adults in general, and other adult women in particular, to form new and supportive alliances. She'd been disappointed by virtually every adult in her life up to that point, and when she got to me, and when I convinced her to open up, she started looking at me as a surrogate parent, the person who had all the answers.

I couldn't be that for her!

In hindsight, I realized I should have used the theater and arts work she and I did to help Kim learn values of self-reliance and confidence, and I should have helped her to learn how to get the best from herself and reach out to other women when the time came to do so. I should have established a mentor relationship with her, rather than a quasi-parental relationship based on my ability to resolve the problems in her life. The parental relationship was doomed to failure, and I should have realized that from the beginning. When Kim's parents dropped off the radar screen and she stopped coming to our center—a development that really shouldn't have come as any surprise to me—I realized that all I had done was to add to Kim's bitterness, cynicism, and mistrust about the outside world that adults lived in.

During the precious time I'd spent with Kim, I hadn't taught her any coping skills in the way my mom and my Aunt Lu had taught me how to reach out to other people at that party. I'd fooled myself into thinking that the curriculum was all that mattered. And I'd tried to comfort her and support her. In so doing, I'd taken on the role of the mother for her—and she'd clung to me desperately. To this day, my heart aches when I think about the path her life may have taken after she suffered the disappointment of being let down by one more vanishing adult. I don't hold myself responsible for all that I imagine may have happened to her, because I know I did the very best I could at the time. But I've never made that mistake with a girl again.

Mothers and fathers worthy of the names have some enduring emotional connection with their children over the course of a lifetime. They offer support and reassurance and may, with work and luck, be able to develop a friendship with an adult child. That's very different from the function the mentor must be willing to take on.

The mentor's role is not to mother a girl who enters her circle. Instead, the mentor must serve as an early—perhaps the first—*adult* relationship outside of the parent/child framework, and must offer strategies for initiating and nurturing more such supportive relationships. Mentors don't pretend that the relationship is going to endure in the long term. Some friendships do last for years, of course, but they're more the exception than the rule. They're a bonus. To be a successful mentor, you must be willing to lay the foundations for a relationship that leads to other relationships, a relationship that teaches girls to open up not just to you, but to the world at large, and to make some sense of that world once you're not around to coach them anymore.

That's a real challenge sometimes, but it is the essence of good mentoring. We are meant to provide our girls with support as they make the transitions that will eventually allow them to support themselves—and reach out to others.

Most of the mentor relationships I've initiated as an adult have come to an end. I had a period of influence, a period that concluded, or at least took on a radically new form, when the girl I was working with passed certain personal thresholds in her life. That's a poignant experience, especially the first few times it occurs. The ideas that follow in this book are meant to help women make the most of the (probably limited) time available to them during the adolescence or young adulthood of some girl who needs help—a girl like you were, a girl like I was, a vulnerable girl. (By the way, I call these people "girls," regardless of their ages, because the technical term, "mentee," always sounds to me like something you'd hear in a science fiction movie.)

You can count on this: When there's a girl in your circle, there's a girl who needs help and support from someone who isn't her mother or father. If you're a parent, my challenge to you is to help your girl find the mentor she needs. If you're a mother, my challenge to you is to find a way to serve as a mentor to some other girl who needs you (perhaps even a friend of your daughter's). And to all women who have benefited from the guiding hands of women who cared for them and helped them find the way, I challenge you to use the ideas that follow in this book to pass along the gift you yourself received as a young person. I challenge you to decide to make a positive difference in the life of a girl who needs you—simply because she is one of our daughters, a daughter of womankind itself.

3

What You Need to Know about Mentoring

If you're a mother, the best thing you can do to help your daughter master the difficult art of growing up is to support her relationship with a mentor whose values reflect your own.

There's simply no doubt that your girl is going to find someone else to connect with when it comes time to deal with the difficult questions and extraordinary challenges that will come her way. The question is: How can you make sure that the people who have an impact on her development will share your values?

Most of the strategies contained in this book are directed toward the person who's there to do the listening when your daughter is confronting new challenges—her mentor. That's not to say, however, that what follows in this book does not concern parents. I believe that the best mentors are those who work hand in hand with active, involved parents.

I also believe that mothers make some of the best mentors, and that they owe it to themselves, their families, and to all of us to learn how to *become* mentors.

One of the best ways for a mother to develop a closer, more meaningful relationship with her own daughter, I've found, is to step forward as the mentor for the daughter's best friend. I cannot recommend this step highly enough. It allows you to reach out to another girl who needs you— and it also helps you to send a powerful message of acceptance for the role your mentor is playing in your own daughter's life.

I encourage parents in general, and mothers in particular, to become familiar with the ideas that appear in the chapters of this book dealing with physical development, intellectual development, emotional development, spiritual development, and financial accountability—the five essentials that form the goals of any working mentor relationship with a girl or young woman. The more you know about what good mentoring looks like, the more likely you will be to offer helpful suggestions and support to the woman or women who act as mentors in your daughter's life. And the more deeply you become involved with the work of mentoring girls other than your daughter, the better you'll understand the challenges both your daughter and her own mentor face. By helping other girls to manage the difficult journey from childhood to adulthood, you'll gain a good understanding of the role the right mentor can play in your own daughter's development.

Think Back

Was there a special woman in your life, someone whom you looked up to, someone who helped you between the ages of roughly nine and eighteen, someone who was not a member of your immediate family? Was there someone you could turn to, someone whose ability to listen, or to offer appropriate constructive criticism, seemed to make all the difference?

When I was in seventh grade, one of the girls at my school made fun of me. She'd reach down the back of my dress, in an attempt to "slingshot" my bra strap; when she found no strap, she let everyone in the line for the bus know that I wasn't wearing a bra. It was a painful experience, and it wasn't made any easier by my mother's previous insistence that I didn't "need" a bra. Whether or not I should have shared all my feelings about this experience with my mother before I shared them with anyone else, I didn't. I sat down with my Aunt Lu and sobbed my way through everything. She listened—which was exactly what I needed—and then gave me a hug and told me not to worry. She said that the people who'd been laughing at me were small-minded, and that in the long run, I'd be all right. She told me that what I was going through was all part of growing up. I could tell that she knew what she was talking about, and that she'd been down the road I was now walking. Somehow, the same message coming from my mother wouldn't have had the same effect. I was able to pull myself together, come to terms with the situation, and move on. That afternoon, my mother and I talked the situation over, and we headed to the department store where, with her help, I bought my first bra.

Aunt Lu helped me make sense of a moment of "passage" in my life. Doesn't your daughter deserve someone who can play the same role? If you stop to think about it, isn't she in need of such a person even more than you were yourself at her age? Aren't the familiar adolescent "traumas"—like my experience at school that day—combined with the potential for much more serious problems for today's girls? Was alcohol abuse as large a problem among teens during your youth as it is for the teens in the world your daughter is entering? Were teen pregnancy rates as high? Were the risks associated with sexually transmitted diseases as alarming? Were family structures as strong? Was divorce as large a factor in people's lives?

Over the last twenty to thirty years, a whole generation of women has come of age with an unprecedented emphasis on career and personal development. It's been an amazing ride, and those of us who have been part of this social revolution have achieved some extraordinary things. But there comes a time when we have to ask, "Is our generation to be the one in which support for the next generation of girls and young women begins to vanish?"

As women, we have to stop and think about what our society is asking girls and young women to handle. Aren't we expecting far more of all our daughters than anyone ever expected of us—and offering them less support than we ourselves received? Right now, in cities and towns across the country, girls are struggling with these challenges, among many others: highly sophisticated media manipulation, uncertain moral standards, self-loathing arising from impossible standards of physical beauty, heavy peer pressure concerning sexuality and substance abuse, and a host of sobering academic and career dilemmas. Who can they turn to for help and guidance? In my view, girls and young women today face hurdles far more daunting than those of virtually any previous generation. They will want to know: "Where is the generation that came before us?"

We must reach out to the daughters of others. After all, if we cannot make time for anyone else's daughter, then who will make time for our daughter?

The Challenge for Mothers

Your daughter has been growing up with you as her model, guide, and advisor. She has learned about the world with your help, and she has experienced both intense emotional connection and powerful conflicts with you. She needs you. But she also needs to grow apart from you. That difficult period when women and young girls are convinced that their parents have nothing of value to add to discussions of key issues is the very period when they are most desperately in need of the insights of a stable mentor figure.

Make no mistake: The mother/daughter bond will remain a dominant force in your daughter's life for as long as she walks on this earth. But as powerful as that relationship is, it's not the only relationship she needs as she approaches adulthood.

In order to forge identities as independent women, we must all move away from the comforting hands and soothing voices that directed us in our younger years. And we must, at the same time, move ahead into new relationships with other women. If we are fortunate, these will be women of wisdom and maturity. From them, we learn, not to do as we are told, but to do what is necessary to make new connections and ongoing growth possible for us as adults.

The years between nine and eighteen are challenging ones for any mother/daughter relationship. Beliefs, values, and interdependence are tested, confronted and questioned in a seemingly endless series of distancing and embracing maneuvers. Some girls develop very close relationships with their mothers during this period—others seem to demand so much "space" and make mothers feel excluded from nearly everything of importance in their daughters' lives. Whether your girl's behavior is on one extreme or the other, or falls somewhere in between, it's important that you understand that her healthy development depends not only on the kind of relationship she has with you, but how she learns to deal with other women.

You will be her mother for as long as you both live, and you will continue to be a crucial role model for years to come. But in order for your daughter to have the best possible chance to learn effective strategies for negotiating the many challenges of adulthood, she needs another role model, another wise woman with whom she can build a peer relationship—perhaps her first peer relationship with another adult. Support that relationship and help your daughter learn to be comfortable when reaching out to wise women for help. Let your daughter see you reach out to other women for support, insight, personal development and career success—and let her see you reach out to her friends as a mentor. By showing that you yourself need support from other women, and that you're willing to give support to girls in your daughter's circle, you'll be helping to support the emergence of one or more strong mentor relationships in her life.

You can help to find the right mentor for your daughter in a number of different ways. Here are some of the best. As you consider these strategies, remember that it is an honor to be asked to take an active role in the life of a girl—and remember, too, that the mentor relationship will work best when your daughter knows that you support and encourage her contacts with this person.

- Reach out to your daughter's aunt. Sisters (or sisters-in-law) may understand and respect your values more fully than anyone else. Take the time to share this book with your daughter's aunt (or grandmother, or other female relative). Reach out. Make the first move—if the person does not yet have children, she may not yet understand the importance of female role models in your daughter's life.

- Reach out to the mother of your daughter's best friend. Mothers can "cross-mentor" each other's girls if there's a sense of shared values and mutual commitment. Again, show the person this book—and emphasize that each of you has an interest in developing good mentor relationships for your girls.

- Reach out to your best friend. I asked my best friend Allie to be my daughter's mentor, and it worked out superbly for everyone. I knew Allie had a set of personal values I could respect, and I knew that Andrea already looked up to her.

- Reach out to your next-door neighbor, especially if she has a girl your daughter's age. Again, both of you share a vested interest in establishing a solid mentor relationship for your girls. Make sure you have a sense of who this person is and what she believes in before you encourage her to play a large role in your daughter's life.

- Reach out to your girl's favorite teacher. And bear in mind that this person is not necessarily her current teacher. Pick out a female classroom teacher (or counselor, or gym instructor, or head of an extracurricular group) who has established a good relationship with your daughter; call her up and ask to have coffee with her. Explore the chemistry between the two of you. Bring this book along. If everything "clicks," ask if the teacher will help you help your daughter by playing a more active role in her life. A good teacher will be happy to consider taking on an expanded role in your girl's life.

- Reach out to social, business, or religious organizations. Women in the Girl Scouts, in your church, mosque, or synagogue, or in an outreach program affiliated with your local college or university often make excellent mentors. Sororities, chambers of commerce, a coworker, your own boss—the possibilities are endless. See the end of this book for a listing of resources that may help you locate mentor candidates outside of family, neighborhood, or school structures.

What is Mentoring?

What is mentoring? Mentoring is stepping forward as a new role model in a girl's life. Mentoring means...

- Listening to help develop or reinforce basic self-esteem

- Encouraging dreams

- Acknowledging nightmares

- Saying "yes" (as in "Yes, you can.")

- Helping girls and young women to develop strategies for communicating with others

- Showing that unfamiliar people and situations are not necessarily hostile people and situations

- Helping girls and young women move beyond their environment—to celebrate what's exciting and vibrant and energetic about it, and to move past what's limiting, abusive, or negative about it

- Exposing girls and young women to new areas of experience—and helping them learn to choose their own "paths least traveled by"

- Demonstrating by example

- Showing girls and young women how to respond to hardships and temporary setbacks

- Learning when to take an (apparently) passive, listening role (because the person you're mentoring needs simple emotional reinforcement, not lectures)

- Learning when to get out front and tell the person you're mentoring to take on a "you can do it" challenge

In the end, mentoring means working with "your girl" on the five essentials:★

- Physical development

- Intellectual development

- Emotional development

- Spiritual development

- Financial accountability

In the pages that follow, there are many different strategies for fostering growth in these five areas. Good mentors shouldn't expect to pursue all of these strategies—but they

---

★ Of course, I don't mean to suggest that boys are not in need of guidance or support in these areas, or that mentorship for boys is unnecessary. The male mentorship experience is a different one, however. For an excellent introduction to the topic of mentorship for boys, see Michael Gurian's fine book *The Wonder of Boys: What Parents, Mentors, and Educators Can Do to Shape Boys into Exceptional Men*, Putnam, 1997.

should certainly make a commitment to work on as many of them as will help to make a positive impact in the life of the girl they're trying to help.

Bear in mind that girls truly want help, even though they can't always put accurate labels on the kind of help they need. Mentors shouldn't expect (and certainly parents shouldn't expect) teenage girls to walk up to them during a calm moment and say something like this:

> *"You know, I've been doing a lot of thinking about where I'm going in my life, and I've decided I really need to get a better handle on my physical sense of well-being. I need to fig-ure out how my sexuality fits into my identity, how to handle these new feelings I'm having, and I also need to take full responsibility for maintaining my body, keeping fit and staying in shape. How do you suppose I ought to go about doing that? Do you have any suggestions? Oh, and some-thing else—I really need to get a handle on emotions and the way they affect the important relationships in my life. I feel like I need some guidance and support in that area, as well. Maybe you've got some suggestions on the best ways for me to make sense of my emotional state on a day-to-day basis, and maybe you could help me focus in on how emotional reactions may be undermining my attempts to formulate meaningful life goals. I also have a nagging feeling I'm not making the smartest money decisions in the world. Maybe you could offer me a little counseling sometime…"*

Girls and young women don't speak out directly about these needs—but that doesn't mean they're not interested in the answers to the dilemmas they face in these areas. They have to be approached in the right way. They have to be approached by someone who is unconditionally supportive, not of specific actions, but of the person's underlying identity. That person has to be a mentor.

A girl's mentor has to be willing, first and foremost, to listen. (That's how mentors prove they're unconditionally supportive. They invest the time it takes to listen meaningfully.) Then, at appropriate points, mentors offer stories from their own lives—examples that say, in essence, "This is how I overcame this problem; maybe that approach will work for you." For reasons that have everything to do with human development, and nothing to do with anyone's failings as a parent, adolescent girls are more likely to listen to that message attentively when it comes from a mentor than when it comes from a parent.

We know how to provide the information these girls need because we've lived life. But we can't *start out* trying to impart the information. We have to be willing to do what's necessary to lay the foundations for a strong relationship. We have to prove that we're willing to listen. Once mentors do that, they virtually always find that the girls and young women they've reached out to are eager for feedback about every goal, every major choice, every life option, every possible strategy.

They're not adults yet, so they can't express their needs in the way an adult might. They're going through a period in their lives when advice from parents in general, and mothers in particular, is viewed with deep suspicion or even outright hostility, regardless of the content or intention of that advice. But their rejection of the kind of advice they took so easily when they were seven or eight does not mean that girls believe they have all the answers.

Girls who need mentors know full well that there's a lot for them to learn. They get compelling evidence of this "knowl edge gap," every day, and it worries them. But it's not easy for them to admit that worry openly to anyone—at least, not at the outset of a relationship. That means someone has to reach out.

In the next chapter, you'll learn how mentors can do that by addressing the first essential element, that of physical development—the foundation of the mentor relationship.

4

The First Essential: Physical Development

Not too long ago, a fifteen-year-old girl in my neighborhood—I'll call her Paula—was trying, without much success, to come to terms with some big problems in her life. Paula was not a happy person.

I knew because I'd seen her tense, defensive face as she walked by our house, and because her mother and I had talked about the academic difficulties she was having at school, the "bad crowd" she was beginning to spend time with, and the turmoil she was experiencing as she struggled to make sense of her own sexuality. Several of Paula's closest friends had been involved in extremely destructive relationships with teenage boys who glorified the gang subculture. I think Paula's mother was concerned that her daughter might be at risk for encountering such problems herself. So her mother reached out to me—a concerned neighbor and friend—and the two of us started talking about what could be done.

Paula's Walk

Paula's mother and I both agreed that we were looking at someone who would benefit from an adult friend, a woman to talk to, an older ally with whom she could feel comfortable communicating on a daily basis. What Paula needed, of course, was a mentor: a woman who wasn't part of the parental structure, but who would be able to listen sensitively and attentively and help her explore all the challenges she faced. I seemed as good a candidate for the role as anyone else. Her mother was confused and depressed, however, at the prospect of my attempting to connect with her daughter. "I know you're what she needs," Paula's mother told me, "but I honestly don't think you can get through to her. She just doesn't want to talk about any of these issues. She'll never discuss what's really bothering her. I know. I've tried for months to get through to her."

And yet, within two weeks, Paula—a girl I had barely spoken to beforehand—had bonded comfortably and completely with me. She had opened up like a flower, volunteering all kinds of sensitive personal information, asking me for guidance on boys, offering insights and frustrations she had about her own body and her image, questioning me on career issues, and, with some help from me, developing realistic strategies for dealing with subjects that were giving her trouble at school.

Paula was asking my advice on all the subjects her mother had been so certain her daughter and I would "never discuss." A month or so after Paula and I had started our talks,

I felt confident that she had taken the steps she needed to take to get her life in order. Paula herself was concerned that her life might take the same disastrous wrong turn her friends' lives had taken, and once she was able to talk through those concerns with me, we were able to set up some strategies that seemed likely to help her maintain the balance, equilibrium, and self-respect she needed to enjoy life.

Her mother was overjoyed—and more than a little perplexed. "How on earth," she asked me, "did you pull that off?" It's a question I've heard from countless mothers over the years.

Paula's turnaround didn't happen because I've got a particularly magnetic personality, or because I have some special ability to hypnotize adolescent girls into doing what I want them to do. It happened because a) I wasn't Paula's mother, and b) I was willing to use an initial contact strategy that incorporates a powerful, understated appeal. This was an appeal that Paula responded to positively in next to no time, and that had nothing to do with lectures, moralizing, or sales pitches of any kind. That initial contact strategy, and its many implications, are what you're going to be reading about in this chapter. It has to do with moving around physically, either on a small or large scale. As you'll see, targeting the activity to the needs, personality, and predisposition of the girl you're working with is absolutely critical.

In Paula's case, the key to getting her to open up to me was simply asking her whether she'd accompany me as I walked my dog around the neighborhood. She agreed, and the ritual soon became the backdrop for a vitally important, steadily deeper relationship between the two of us. During those walks, Paula felt safe, supported, and (before too long) challenged in a positive, nurturing way. She shared things with me that she'd never have shared with her mother. I'd be willing to bet that she listened to me in a way she'd never listened to her mother.

It all began when I walked up to her on the street and said, "Hey—do you want to go for a walk with me? My dog needs to get some exercise, and I could use some company."

I actually didn't have to talk her into anything. She accepted my invitation as though it was a life preserver and held on for all she was worth. Some girls will respond quickly to a mentor's overtures, as Paula did. Others will need a little more persistence.

There was, of course, a great deal more going on between Paula and me than a commitment to walk the dog together. She may not have been able to discuss it in such terms at the time, but Paula had signed on for a course in Adulthood, 101—of her own volition.

I would love to be able to say that simply walking up to a girl and asking for her help in walking the dog is all that's necessary to turn around her life. The truth is, though, that there's a much more complex set of forces at work; mentors need to be able to harness them and respond appropriately to them if they expect to make a real difference.

Let's assume, from this point of the book onward, that you're a mentor, someone who wants to connect with a girl and make a positive difference in her life. In this chapter, you'll learn why my outreach strategy with Paula worked, what you can do to adapt it to the circumstances you and your girl face, and how to follow through when the girl you are offering attention to eventually responds positively. (Trust me —she will.)

Why Bother?

In our society it's very easy to decide not to take on vigorous (or even not-so-vigorous) physical activity. Many of the people who come to my seminars think of physical activity as identical to "exercise," and categorize it as something that would be nice to work into their relationships with girls, if circumstances allow. The truth is that physical activity is not an "optional" part of reaching out to your girl. It's an essential part of the process, and I believe a good argument can be made that no meaningful mentor relationship is possible without some form of shared physical activity between you and the girl you're trying to help. The good news is, that in the early going, physical activity can be quite modest and may look nothing like what you're used to thinking of as "exercise." The more challenging news, if you're among the millions of people in this society for whom a physical workout is not a regular event, is that, eventually, you must help your girl feel and see herself succeeding in some form of vigorous physical activity. What's more, you must be by her side, sharing in that activity, pushing yourself just as hard as you're challenging her to push herself.

You're not out to focus your girl on winning or losing, but on the act of doing something challenging with her body—on taking the steps, and, with your help, doing more with that body than she once thought was possible. (In the process, you will, in all likelihood, have to do something with your body that you hadn't thought possible, or at least likely.)

But I'm getting ahead of myself. How, exactly, does physical activity serve as an entry point in the relationship?

Bodies in Motion

The act of using one's body to open up a new relationship with a girl who needs mentoring is the first skill any good mentor needs to master. There's absolutely no sexual component to this type of reaching out, and you certainly don't have to be in perfect shape to make this appeal work. In fact, the relationship will probably deepen more quickly if you have a meaningful goal of your own—such as a specific, reasonable weight-loss target—to shoot for as a "workout partner." The aim is not to further glorify unattainable media-driven standards for physical beauty. The aim is, instead, to show how a real woman takes aim at a real, sensible target. You're out to use your own body to focus the natural power of shared physical action. That mutual action will help to lower your girl's initial defenses against new people and experiences. It will also demonstrate that you truly want to listen and help, and, eventually, challenge her to overcome her own fears and demand the very best from herself.

Women of all shapes and sizes can use the ideas in this chapter to reach out to, and help build up self-esteem in, the girls they're trying to help. As a matter of fact, I'd venture to guess that mentors who do not reflect the conventional, and limited, "model-of-the-month" notion of physical beauty have a slight edge in effectiveness over mentors who do. (Some girls may feel intimidated by mentors who seem "impossibly" beautiful, although a sensitive, caring mentor can usually overcome even this obstacle.)

The initial outreach via physical activity can take many forms, but as you will see, it can and must eventually move forward into a meaningful commitment to physical fitness and exercise goals. You don't have to be the world's greatest athlete to help your girl. But you do have to be able to use your body in some kind of appropriate, escalating physical activity that will help your girl accept her own physicality and learn more about:

- your role as someone who's willing to listen and not lecture;

- healthy body image development;

- the importance of regular exercise;

- specific issues of physical change and development;

- and, perhaps most important of all, mental attitude in the face of adversity—physical and otherwise.

As you work with your girl to attain physical goals, you will find that she will often take the initiative in discussing these and other important issues with you.

You need to be able to show your girl the steps she needs to take when she feels as though it's time to give up. It's not feeling discouraged that's the problem for so many of today's girls—it's a lack of first-hand observation about what to do when that feeling arises! When your girl reaches a point in her life when she's thinking to herself...

- I can't understand this homework assignment

- I can't be successful in college

- I don't think I'm smart enough to make it through

- I don't think I'm pretty enough to make it though

- I don't think I'm tough enough to make it through

- I can't handle this

- I'm going to give up

...your goal is to help her mental dialogue to proceed in a constructive way from that point, and you're going to use physical activity to do that. It's not a question of whether thoughts like these are going to cross her mind—it's a question of when they will, and what choices, empowering or life-shattering, your girl will make when the stakes are the highest.

When she says those things to herself, she has to be able to see that she has inner resources that will guide her through the tough times. It's not enough to *tell* her to develop those inner resources. It's not even enough to remind her constantly that they're there for her to develop whenever she wants to. She has to be walked through—literally, walked or biked or hiked through—the process of calling on the deepest part of herself. And her mentor—the person I'll be addressing as "you" from this point on in the book—has to be the one who initiates the physical actions that make her "success response" a reality.

This is not a theoretical exercise in positive thinking. It's a tangible, physical reality for survival conditioning. I believe that this only takes hold effectively when a nonparental role model steps in at some relatively early point in the girl's development and establishes some routine involving physical activity or challenge. That routine doesn't have to be formalized—but it does have to have you at its center, and it has to be carefully targeted to the girl's situation and personality.

In the final analysis, the most important obstacle any girl faces is fear. Fear of the outside world, fear of herself, fear that she won't be able to meet the standards that others set for her, fear that she will be inadequate on some level. I believe that faith is the opposite of fear—and that faith in oneself, although it is a hard-won commodity, can be brought about via a series of shared physical actions. In this chapter, you're going to learn how to make faith and high self-esteem realities for the girl who's counting on you by reaching out to her through a physical activity.

Initially, the activities I'm talking about can be as simple as taking a brisk walk as part of a daily exercise regimen, strolling around an amusement park together, or even engaging in some form of arts and crafts work. Whether you're walking around and going on rides together or creating something together, you're opening yourselves up to the possibility of discovering new experiences together.

Careful!

It's great to set physical goals, but the attainment of them is not the main issue here. Do not mistake physical outreach for the "shape up or ship out" approach, where you attempt to instill yourself as a fitness instructor or other authority figure. That's a major turnoff, especially at the outset of the relationship. What you're after is a shared base of experiences as the prelude to, and the foundation for, a relationship—a friendship. This friendship will feature its share of challenges, but it should not be defined by those challenges (or by, for instance, potentially unhealthy intimidation about the necessity of weight loss). Instead, the friendship should be defined by the experiences you and your girl make sense of side by side.

The more experiences a girl has shared with you, the more likely she is to pass along the important thoughts and questions she has. Sometimes, your girl will be so eager to build up an alliance with you that only one or two shared experiences will be necessary to encourage her to talk openly with you. But those experiences must take place first, and they must have some physical component, even a very modest one. After only a few walks together, Paula came to think of me as one of her closest friends—but we had to share the experience of walking together a few times for us to reach that point.

Once your girl starts opening up, you'll start to get a picture of who this person is, what she values, and what she wants to find out from you. You'll also learn how she thinks about the world around her, which is one of the most important breakthroughs any mentor can make.

Virtually every girl you meet already has the tools she needs to negotiate the passage from childhood to maturity. But she needs to interact with you to learn where those tools are and how to use them. She needs to see you in action—coping. And that's what physical activity does. It gives your girl an opportunity to share in your world in a tangible, sensory way and learn first-hand how you respond to challenges.

The Roller Coaster

Sometimes you can start a mentor relationship almost without knowing it. Recently, my friend Debbie went on a family trip with her niece Caroline. They went to Epcot Center in Florida; Caroline's mom had been a little nervous about taking part in some of the more adventurous rides, so Debbie volunteered to accompany Caroline. They had fun together, of course—but there was also a certain special kind of physical bonding taking place, the kind of bonding that can only happen when you undertake a physical challenge with someone and experience your heart pumping fast, your eyes widening, and your breath rate increasing. By climbing on that ride with Debbie, Caroline was sharing a moment of heightened, nonsexual physical awareness with an older woman and building a deeper bond with her in the process.

Caroline and Debbie could have started the process with some form of physical activity that didn't increase the heart rate (such as needlework or sketching). In their case, however, the means by which they started to connect with each other more deeply was exhilarating. As a general rule, connections are stronger and deeper when you engage your girl in a shared undertaking that moves you both into another level physically. If she's willing to take on such an activity, you should go for it. That's not to say that the initial activity should leave you both exhausted; you'll probably want to work your way up to that! I'm talking about the kinds of activities you can share together briefly and experience a light physical "buzz" of some kind. At the end of the activity, you look at each other and say, "Wow—that was interesting, wasn't it?"

I call these strategies for initial physical contact "low-intensity buzzes." They get your blood pumping—but they're not going to be confused with a marathon run or a hike up a major mountain.

These activities could include:

- A light workout

- A ride at a go-kart center

- A visit to a bowling alley

- A brisk walk around the block

- A modest jog

- A trip on a roller coaster or other ride

- A modest canoe trip

- A modest hike

- A short foot race

Why It Works

This initial, shared exploration of physicality can have a truly powerful bonding effect on both you and the girl to whom you're reaching out. I've personally experienced this more times than I can count.

One reason this powerful experience comes about as easily as it does has to do with the undeniable—and pleasant!—act of overcoming fear by means of shared physical action. Doing things together is less scary than doing them alone. This idea applies to canoeing or amusement park rides in a fairly obvious way, but the same growth is also present in more subtle ways when a girl simply tries to overcome a long-running mental block against exercise or communication with others. The act of taking on a physical activity together allows us to participate emotionally with the girl in question.

When we share important physical experiences with girls, we also share important emotional experiences with girls. Shared physical action makes it easier for girls to overcome their fears, and it allows us to show them how a relationship with a mature (but not perfect!) adult can make the process of personal growth a good deal easier.

I want to emphasize here that you, as the mentor, are not entering the relationship as the "expert"—a role that can change with disconcerting speed into that of the surrogate parent. You're nothing like a parent. You're a friend who's willing to take on exactly the same activity your girl will be experiencing. You're not offering critiques and stepping back. You're participating fully in the experience with your girl and sharing it with her as one friend shares with another.

You're not in charge of anything. You're there to listen and observe—at least in the early going.

After her experience on the roller coaster at Epcot, Debbie learned a great deal about how Caroline dealt with her own emotions—how she handled her own life. The roller coaster ride served as a microcosm of sorts, an object lesson in how this young lady interacted, not just with the specific physical challenge of the roller coaster, but with a whole range of other challenges as well. She took deep breaths before she got on the roller coaster, for instance, which indicated that she already had a certain amount of "built-in" stress management training. She was a very protective person. She found reasons to comfort Debbie during the course of the ride. She'd say, "It's okay—breathe deep, let it go, and you'll be fine."

Debbie appealed to this habit of Caroline's a month or so later. The two had become quite close, and Caroline was visiting one afternoon, talking about how afraid she was of taking on a particularly challenging math class. After listening (and remember, that's rule number one—truly listening) to Caroline's concerns about the challenges this class represented, Debbie was able to say, "Hey, remember that time we were together on the roller coaster? You said to me to take a deep breath and just relax—that it was going to be a little scary at first, but that afterwards, when everything was all over, I was going to be fine. I think this class could be a lot like that."

Now that's not a lecture. That's not a set of furrowed eyebrows accompanied by a serious talk about how Caroline "has to do better at school." It's help from a friend, based on a shared experience. That gets a much better reaction from a girl than a lecture.

A lecture gets you "Yeah, right, okay," and it doesn't penetrate. A parallel like the one Debbie made after the roller coaster ride, one that appeals to the girl's existing set of survival and coping skills, isn't perceived as outside instruction. It's an extension of something that already works.

That kind of encouragement from a mentor makes the girl's eyes light up; she says, or, more important, feels, "Aaahhhh—I get it." What's more, this kind of observation has the effect of bringing you and the girl closer together—and making more such moments possible in the future. At its best, I think mentoring is a process that allows girls to watch you cope and encourages them to summon resources and aptitudes that already exist within themselves.

Shared physical challenges—modest or dramatic—make it abundantly clear to your girl that you're not there simply to give (unsought) advice, but to take part in a mutually rewarding relationship in which both of you grow.

Getting Started

"Let's take a walk."

Whether you're visiting your niece, heading up a girl scout troop that has one particularly withdrawn scout, or reaching out to the girl next door, these experiences can be an incredibly effective means of initiating contact. Just pick up the phone and ask the girl (or her mother or father) about the possibility of getting a little fresh air together. If you're reaching out to a neighbor with whom you already have a good relationship, this will be relatively easy. If you have yet to introduce yourself fully to the family, you'll probably want to suggest that a parent tag along for the first excursion. But basically, the message to the girl you're trying to help is a simple one:

- "Hey, it's a beautiful day (or evening)—let's get out and do some walking."

- "I've got an exercise routine going; I have to get in half a mile of walking a day, and it's so much more fun when I do it with someone else. Want to come with me?"

- "I've got to walk my dog Gus after work—want to keep us company tonight?"

- "I've got an hour to kill—I was wondering if you wanted to walk up to Route 114 with me. I work at home, and it's the best way I can think of to break up the routine and put a little exercise in the middle of the day."

So you start walking with the girl. Or perhaps you've decided on a bike ride or some other shared activity. I'll assume that you're walking together, since that's one of the easiest and among the most accessible types of exercise. (The suggestions that follow can be adapted without too much difficulty to a whole range of "low-intensity buzzes.")

Usually the opening few moments of the relationship are quiet ones. That's okay. You're walking. She's walking. You haven't done much (or anything) together yet, so there's not really much to talk about. You just keep the rhythm of your legs and arms going. Your body is moving along, getting used to the beat the two of you are establishing. Her body is doing the same thing. That's enough to occupy both of you for a while.

Don't be afraid of silence! It's better than moralizing or attempting to lay down ground rules at the outset of the relationship.

Five or ten minutes go by, and the two of you now do have a shared experience. You've walked together for a fair distance. Perhaps you start to break the silence now by offering your own "soundtrack" to the proceedings. Again, you shouldn't do this right away—give yourselves the time and opportunity to develop a shared rhythm first.

One of my favorite approaches to setting up a "soundtrack" once a girl and I are walking in synch is to sing—on my own initiative, and without any request that the girl join in. I'll just start quietly singing some of the songs we sang when I was a kid: Beatles songs, say. ("Mother Nature's Son" or "Dear Prudence" tend to work pretty well.) Maybe your girl joins in. Maybe she doesn't. Either way, it's okay. You've taken the initiative; you've put yourself out there a little bit. You've shown a side of yourself to her without demanding anything in return.

You say you're not the singing kind? That's no problem— although I should note that there may be no better way to let someone else know that you're willing to lower your guard than to voluntarily share your out-of-key singing with them. Still, there's no reason to try to sing to yourself if doing so makes you extremely uncomfortable.

Another great strategy to take the pressure off your girl is simply to offer, five or ten minutes into your walk, your observations on your surroundings. Say something about the flowers you're passing. Or the snow. Or the weather. Or the construction site up ahead. Don't demand any response from your girl; don't expect her to agree with you or amplify anything you say. Just make your own observation and let it hang there in the air for a bit. Make it clear that you're willing to carry the social weight of the encounter on your own shoulders, as it were.

Again: You must open up without pressuring your girl to provide information, share insights or feelings, or to offer any information whatsoever. Make a comment: "The azaleas are out—they look really beautiful." Then let it fade, and make it clear that you're just as comfortable with silence as you are with conversation. If you're walking a dog—a great "starter" walk, by the way—you can offer occasional comments on what the dog usually does, how he or she reacts to strangers, where you got him, and so on.

After a few minutes of non-threatening song and/or conversation—in other words, after you've made it perfectly clear that this really is a pleasant occasion, and not an opportunity for you to launch some sinister initiative or other—you can start asking some non-threatening questions that elicit feelings and/or insights from the girl you're walking with. (She may well have started to pitch in with her own ideas and observations at this point, but just in case she hasn't, you should be ready with some questions of your own.)

Appropriate questions to ask once you've made it clear that you're not out to spy, harass, berate, or interrogate your girl could sound like this:

- "Wow—look at that flower—isn't that beautiful?"

- "Have you ever had any pets?"

- "Have you ever been up this way before?"

- "So what do you think of the neighborhood? Do you like living here?"

- "What kind of work does your mom/dad do?"

After a few such questions, you'll almost certainly find, as you continue walking forward purposefully and contentedly (or engaging in whatever other physical activity the two of you have selected), that your girl will start asking questions of her own or sharing opinions at some length. She may start discussing her other friends, or a recent event at school, or even something that's happening in her own home. Those first few minutes of investment in the relationship—the time you take to demonstrate that you aren't out to ask personal questions or deliver moral lessons to someone that you hardly know—really pay off, often in very short order.

By taking the initiative to begin conversation, and by beginning it in a neutral, open way, I have had the (extraordinary!) experience of listening to supposedly "withdrawn" girls start to open up about the most private parts of their lives during the very first talk. You can too, although most mentors find that it takes a few physical encounters to build up enough shared experience to make this possible.

Who knows, though? You may well find that the girl will start to talk about a friend at school who doesn't like walking—or perhaps she'll mention a friend who has an eating disorder or recently had an abortion. That's right, these "I know someone who..." references can and do come up during the very first prolonged discussion period. Why? Because you've established yourself—in just a few minutes—as an impartial, mature, and trustworthy adult. "I know someone who..." discussions can function as actual summaries of experiences she's observed that puzzle or confuse her—or they may well reflect questions the girl has about events in her own life that she's not yet comfortable addressing on a first-person basis. In some cases—situations where the girl feels a strong bond with you right off the bat—she will start talking about something that's come up regarding her parents or her family life. Perhaps she complains that her parents don't do something she thinks they ought to be doing, or perhaps she feels her privacy is being invaded.

Whatever you hear, whenever you hear it, remember that your job is to listen, not to judge. The girl's first decision to open up to you is a great time to not say anything.

The girl has responded positively to you. She's followed your lead, responded to your requests to get together. She's listened as you've volunteered your own opinions about (innocuous) subjects in a non-threatening, risk-free manner. In other words, she's trusted you. She's concluded that you really are interested in hearing about what she's up against and knows that you're not likely to react with instantaneous moral judgments about her own thoughts, fears, and emotions.

So she's decided to open up to you—if not on the very first discussion, then at some point shortly thereafter.

If you abuse that trust, the girl will shut down and may regard her decision to trust an adult who has attempted to reach out to her as a serious mistake. If you start spouting platitudes and outlining black-and-white moral guidelines the moment she starts speaking frankly about sensitive issues like weight, peer pressure, drug or alcohol abuse, or sex, then your attempts to develop a meaningful long-term mentor relationship with this girl are probably doomed.

So don't talk. Play it cool. Nod attentively as your girl talks herself through the situation she herself has raised. Listen. Even if what you hear shocks or offends or alarms you, fight the instinct to offer advice or pass judgment—fight those urges with every fiber of your being. Don't get rattled. Just listen. That's the only way you can count on developing the kind of relationship where you're able to make a difference in the long run.

Allow the girl to share exactly what's on her mind. Don't speak up unless and until she asks you a direct question about a matter of importance to her. In most cases, that won't happen until the girl has "vented" for a while. Let her vent. By the way, if a girl does ask you a critical question in the early going, give the best short honest answer you're capable of framing, and then encourage her to continue sharing her feelings and experiences. In the early going— during the first one, two, or three encounters with your girl—the aim is simply to let the girl know that you're there for her, and that you will not render judgment on her feelings or activities for any reason.

Keep walking (or working out, or jogging, or whatever). Don't be alarmed by occasional pauses. Let there be pauses. The girl may feel most comfortable when she lets some time pass between her observations. Enjoy the environment the two of you are sharing together—whether it's a country road, a gym, a hill, a mountain, or even an amusement park— and let it take over the conversation from time to time. This is not a therapy session. It's an opportunity to spend time together comfortably.

Take a moment now to review the outline for your first few meetings with your girl:

- Make the first move by asking the girl to go on a walk (or engage in some other physical activity).

- Don't pressure the girl at the beginning of your session. Establish a shared physical rhythm, and don't be afraid of silence.

- Once you've established a shared rhythm, take the initiative by offering innocuous comments or observations—but don't pressure the girl to make talk for the sake of making talk.

- After a few more moments, be prepared to ask a few non-threatening questions about how the girl feels about the surroundings, the neighborhood, or some other topic that's clearly "neutral."

How to Respond

Some girls take a while to open up. Others will start sharing important information with you with breathtaking speed. Regardless of the personality and background of the girl you've hooked up with, if you follow the guidelines I've set out here, you will almost certainly notice that your girl will eventually—and before too terribly long—start volunteering important facts about her friends, her own life, her family, and the major choices she's facing right now—about sex, about careers, about drugs, about the future—about whatever is Topic A on her personal agenda right now.

It's true that some girls have such serious personal challenges in their history that they may have great difficulty reaching out to you in the early going. I'll look at a strategy you can use to reach such girls a little later in this chapter. In most cases, though, your girl wants to get to the phase in which she can share important information with you—so let her.

She may begin the process by making some (seemingly) simple reference to your own career, your life, or your husband. This is not an invitation for you to ramble on about yourself, or talk at length about a personal problem of your own. At least in the early going, you should respond to such conversational openings briefly, concisely, and openly. Then return the social "ball" to your girl. Don't clam up— but don't act as though you're a talk-show host whose responsibility it is to fill any and all "dead air." If she wants to talk, let her talk. If she wants to focus on the physical activity you're both engaged in, let her do that.

I've seen it happen too many times to think otherwise. Girls open up when they know they've hooked up with a mentor who's truly willing to listen.

So listen. And let your girl talk, or not talk, as her mood suggests.

The Counselor's Dilemma

Therapists, counselors and others who work with kids sometimes wonder why they don't get good results from their one-on-one encounters with troubled girls. I've got a theory: sitting down for long periods of time is a lousy way to begin a mentor relationship! Why? Because girls invariably have one or both of two common reactions to their interactions with these authority figures.

a) The girl may think, "This is boring." She asks herself, "I gave up an afternoon for this?" She goes to a room, she sits down, and she stares at a person who stares right back at her and, all too often, asks questions that are uninformed, unpleasant, or a combination of the two. How would you respond if a stranger started asking you whether you'd been sexually active recently? After the third or fourth dodge, this gets incredibly dull. No matter how good one's interpersonal skills are, no matter how powerful the signals of support, no matter how well intentioned the counselor or therapist may be, the stark fact remains—today's young people are used to being entertained when they sit for long periods of time. And they're used to having a remote control device in their hand as they're being entertained! If girls can't change the channel, they may shut down internally. Without physical activity of some kind, girls (and boys, for that matter) get restless almost immediately.

b) The girl may feel, "I'm on the spot." And why shouldn't she? A fair number of counselors come across—unintentionally—as power trippers. Another group—somewhat smaller, I'd like to believe—intentionally comes across as power trippers. Either way, the result is (at least from the girl's perspective) a barrage of unrequested advice. That's not much fun, and it's highly unlikely to get girls to open up. A good percentage will assume they're being attacked verbally—even though the attacks may not sound insulting or invasive to an outsider. Some of these perceived attacks arise because the counselor or therapist is experiencing a very natural human phenomenon: discomfort with silence. As we've seen, physical activity allows both the girl and her conversational partner to focus on a neutral pursuit when words run dry, which is much less intimidating than the "back-to-the-business-at-hand" tone too many "guidance" professionals assume. After all, they're there to guide—and how can they do that if they're not talking about what the girl ought to be doing? Unfortunately, that approach leads to hostility and resentment from girls. They're much more likely to respond well to some physical activity that leaves them in control of the conversational agenda.

The key is using the body. Many motivational trainers, including world-famous success coach Anthony Robbins, have pointed out the strong correlation between control of one's emotional state and a decision to change one's physical postures and movements. In other words, if you're looking for a good way to help your girl feel as though she's in control of her situation, help her to take direct physical action that's uplifting, engaging, motivating. This body action can take any number of forms, but it should eventually involve some phase in which there is uplift—a walk with one's chest held high, or a bike ride during which one is forced to focus upwards and forward. That upward focus works magic when it comes to instilling focus and confidence and a sense of well being.

A friend of mine has a two-year-old—when she cries over something, he instructs his daughter to look upward: up at a bird in the sky, up at a patch of color on the ceiling, up at an imaginary flying saucer. It never fails: the act of looking up causes his daughter to stop crying, and her outlook improves. I'm not saying you should try to keep your girl from crying by shouting that she look up at the sky, but I am saying, that as you take on your physical activity together, you should strongly consider finding one that incorporates some kind of uplift or upward forward motion.

If Your Girl Won't or Can't Take a Walk, Use Modest Indoor Physical Activity to Reach Her

Some girls, for whatever reason, will not be good candidates for the "low-intensity buzz" activity I've just outlined. Perhaps your girl has a physical disability of some kind, or a serious behavioral problem that makes dropping a "tough" facade and accepting your help extremely difficult. Perhaps your girl has not been served well by the educational, welfare, or criminal justice system.

Even so, you can find a way to use physical activity to launch a good relationship. Again, when I talk about exercise in the early phase of the relationship, I mean the "low-intensity buzz," which involves getting arms and legs pumping and heartbeats rising. But that's not the only strategy available to you.

Arts and crafts work is another physical activity that can help you lay the foundations for a good relationship. And it's an excellent backup if you're trying to reach out to a girl who is extremely resistant to any form of physical workout or who has a disability that makes walking, biking, hiking, or any of the other activities unrealistic. Arts and crafts also represent a good way to reach out to girls who may be in deep trouble—but who have serious mental hurdles that prevent them from reaching out to anyone.

Working on arts and crafts enables girls to take on physical action—usually involving hand-eye coordination. That activity makes the conversation easier, in much the same way that pumping your arms and moving your legs with a girl takes so much of the stress out of an initial contact. There's a *reason* for your meeting, one that doesn't involve you analyzing or judging the girl.

Melanie's Story

When I was interning as a social work student, I was assigned a teenage girl who, by virtue of her family background, was at a very high risk for later problems like early pregnancy and drug abuse. She was fourteen. I'll call her Melanie.

Our first meeting took place some years ago—it was long before I learned about the virtues of heading out for a walk together. The guidelines of the group where I was working were such that there was one and only one way to "counsel" girls in trouble. You sat down in a room and tried somehow to encourage them to talk to you.

For our first session, I had prepared myself to the hilt. I'd read every article, seen every case study, and talked to every person I could track down who had had any experience in dealing with girls whose life experiences mirrored Melanie's. I was ready to listen, ready to engage her, ready to do anything and everything I could to encourage her to start down the path that would eventually lead to a "meaningful conversation" with her.

I took my place in the room. (It was quite an ugly little reception area, as I remember.) She walked in. She sat down. I said hello. She looked at me. She looked away.

Nothing.

Absolute silence. Five minutes passed. Then ten. Then fifteen.

I was horrified. This was not the way this sort of thing was supposed to go. But it was the only way it could go, since I had been assigned to listen, not to talk, and all of my training had been to find ways to help support her in saying whatever it was she wanted to say. (By the way, anyone who knows me will attest that silence is not exactly my strong suit—but, when it's part of the job, it's part of the job.) I was there to listen. So that's what I was going to do.

But Melanie didn't want to say anything. She simply didn't want to talk to me. I was getting more and more nervous and fearful and confused about how badly our first encounter seemed to be going. A hundred different questions were going through my head. What could I do to fill up the silence? Why didn't she like me? Would we ever be able to relate to one another about anything? Could I actually make a difference in her life? Had I done the right thing by showing up for work that morning instead of staying in bed all day long? Had I done the right thing by deciding to go into social work? All kinds of interesting questions were rumbling around my head as that silence stretched on. Most of all, I was thinking, "How can I get her involved with me?" And yet there I was, sitting in this room with this young girl, both of us perched atop this awful extended silence that simply would not end.

The hour concluded. Leaving aside my initial greeting, neither of us had said a word. I said goodbye and told Melanie I'd look forward to getting together with her during our next session the following week. She said nothing and walked out the door.

As tough as it was, I think it was important for me to ride that silence through with Melanie. I had to show her that I was there for her—but I couldn't begin the relationship by pleading with her to talk to me. Nor could I start out by challenging her or subjecting her to interrogation. I remember thinking to myself that this was a girl who had been let down by many, many people in her life. I wanted to show her that I was willing to stick with her, no matter what. Even though the experience was an agonizing one, I went away feeling that I'd earned a measure of respect from her.

All the same, that hour of silence wasn't anything I wanted to repeat if I could avoid doing so.

As the week passed before our next meeting, I tried to think about how I'd feel if I were in Melanie's situation—if my home life were falling apart, and my parents both had serious substance abuse problems and run-ins with the law, and this strange lady had been assigned to sit down in a room with me and find out all about me. I realized that I'd feel pressured, intimidated, and more than a little over-whelmed. I thought, well, that's not much fun. No wonder she's not looking forward to talking to me. Then I asked myself, "Well, what did I like doing when I was a teenager? What was important to me back then?"

I thought about that for a while. Then I thought to myself that, rather than sitting without doing anything for another hour, I should try to find some way to work those activities that I used to enjoy into our next meeting. At the same time, I knew that I wanted to develop skills that would work, not just with Melanie, but with lots of other teens and young girls who faced challenges like the ones she was facing.

So I thought about the kinds of things that motivated me when I was Melanie's age, and then I went shopping.

I bought a big pile of teen magazines (like *Seventeen*), and a bunch of different women's magazines (like *Working Woman* and *Glamour* and *Ms.*). I bought some glue and some big sheets of construction paper. And I bought nail polish—the nice, cheap, ninety-nine cent variety. There were five or six different colors. When my meeting with Melanie came around, I just sat down and waited for her by leafing through the magazines. She walked in. I looked up, smiled, and kept on leafing through the magazines.

More silence—but I could tell somehow that she was more curious than she had been the last time we got together. After a minute or two, I pulled out a pair of scissors and started cutting out pictures from the magazines, pictures that summed up, for me, what it felt like to be a teenager. I started cutting and gluing the images onto the construction paper, based on my own memories of the experience.

She just sat there. But now she had something to look at, an activity to evaluate. Eventually (wonder of wonders!) she asked me what I was doing. And I told her. I said, "I'm cutting out pictures that remind me of what it was like to be a teenager—the things that made a difference to me then, and the things I liked doing then."

At that point, she started shuffling through some of the magazines herself, and she began to leaf through them non-committally. She seemed to be saying, that if I was willing to do something as silly as play kindergarten games with paper and scissors and glue, then the least she could do was take a look at the material I was using. (By the way, this initial reaction of detached tolerance is similar to the way girls react when you start singing to yourself while you're taking a walk with them, or even when you first try to reach out by saying, "Hey, want to help me walk the dog?" They don't exactly want to show their interest in such unusual activities, but they want to find a way to participate with someone who's invested in the activity in such an unusual way.)

Melanie kept looking through the magazines for a few minutes. Notice that, even though it wasn't something that was likely to raise her heart rate or respiration, this was something physical that she could do—something that didn't require any verbal interplay that she wasn't comfortable with or prepared for. Looking through the magazines didn't require any advance study. It didn't require any interpretation. It didn't seem risky. It was a physical activity that allowed her to enter into a shared undertaking with me without any up-front investment in the emotional weight that always seems to accompany a "first conversation."

After a few minutes of leafing through the magazine, Melanie actually weighed in with an opinion: "This picture reminds me of something I did with my mother a couple of years ago." And with that, she started talking about her relationship with her mother. Then she went back to leafing through the magazines. After a while she found another picture, which got her talking about the kinds of challenges she faced, the opportunities she wished she'd had, and what she hoped to see happen in her life. After another period of silently reviewing her magazine, she reached for the second pair of scissors on the table (I'd left them out prominently, but I hadn't shoved them in front of her face). Melanie started clipping and talking, clipping and talking.

That's how the rest of that second meeting went. We'd flip through the magazines. We'd find something interesting. She'd say something about her background. Then we'd flip through the magazines in silence for a while, and the cycle would start all over again. But with every new image, she opened up to me a little bit more, and I could tell she was feeling more comfortable about sharing her feelings with me.

We started making a big collage—and we started giggling. I won't even try to express to you the sense of relief

I felt when that happened, after the trauma and doubt I'd felt during our first hour together the previous week.

The glue was sticking to our fingers. The scissors were getting all sticky, too. The people in the pictures in the magazines were suddenly friends, allies, patient supporters of the cause of our reaching out to one another. Before we knew it, the hour was over—and we hadn't even gotten to the nail polish I'd brought and left out on the table.

Melanie was eager to find out the details of our next meeting. She wanted to know—Would I bring back more magazines next week? Would I bring back more glue, more paper, the scissors? Would I bring back the nail polish so we could give that a try, too? I told her I'd be happy to do all those things.

Suddenly there was a relationship. It wasn't based on my "interviewing" her or (worse still) "probing" her for facts about her life—it was based on mutual trust and discovery. Suddenly I had a friend, and Melanie had a friend. That came about because I took the initiative, and because I took the pressure off her by doing something a little unusual. At the same time, I was using physical activity—in this case, the act of clipping out photographs from magazines—as a means of changing the dynamic of the encounter. Once I introduced an activity, Melanie knew that I wasn't there to "probe" her, or intrude on her life, or make her justify her experiences or priorities in any way.

The awkward silence became a relationship about what we could do, together, with our own hands, sitting across the table from one another in that ugly little room. And that shift allowed Melanie to enter in as a participant in the relationship safely and without precondition.

Melanie's story illustrates powerfully how taking appropriate physical action together is one of the very best—and, I would argue, first—steps a mentor can take to make a positive impact in a girl's life. Appropriate physical action also enables you to relax and accept what does (or doesn't) come along from your girl. Perhaps most important of all, appropriate physical activity allows your girl the option of silence—when she wants it and for however long she wants it—as the relationship progresses. That's something that can't always be said of a girl's relationship with her parents, or (as in Melanie's case) of her relationships with counselors or therapists.

Show that you're not afraid of the silence your girl defines. Let her come to count on it. Let her know it's there for her—and that you accept that it can be just as profound as anything either you or your girl might decide to say.

Using Physical Action to Deal with Your Own Feelings of Nervousness

Focusing on a physical activity makes it easier for the mentor, too. Let's face it—knowing what to say can be difficult. Being able to turn your attention to something you're doing with your hands, or to a brisk walk, or to the dog the two of you are walking, will help you dispel some of your own nervousness and get past that awkward initial phase.

That's another great reason to use something that involves physicality, because it helps you transcend feelings of emotional vulnerability, just as it does for the girl you're mentoring.

Physical activity—whether it's making a collage or setting out on a hike—helps you explore your own values and morals and points of view more fully and more easily. It takes your conscious mind off the "serious stuff" for a moment—and, in a delicious irony, leaves you better equipped to discuss the "serious stuff" when the opportunity arises to do so. And, of course, physical activity helps you to establish a base of shared experiences with your girl.

There's another big advantage for you when you initiate contact with your girl by means of some kind of physical action. Sustained movement with a girl you're mentoring often acts as a kind of time machine. It can bring you back to the time when you yourself were a teenager. That's certainly what my little magazine experiment with Melanie did, and I've had the same rush of recognition at the power and vitality of youth while hiking, biking, walking, and jogging with any number of mentors. I think you'll encounter much the same experience while participating in physical activities you undertake with your girl—either at the beginning of the relationship or later on. It's a remarkable feeling—one that will help you to marshal additional energy for the attainment of your own physical goals, however you identify them.

"Just Do It"

In most cases, you can initiate the listening process by suggesting a walk or a similar "low-intensity buzz" activity. If you face unusual circumstances, you may find that something like clipping pictures is the best way to move forward with your girl.

Whatever you do, you'll be listening—and building up your emotional bond with the girl. As the relationship deepens, you're going to do something sneaky. You're going to try to formalize (or, in the case of arts and crafts contacts, upgrade) your physical routine with the girl. Your aim is to instill a regular routine of low-intensity walking, hiking, biking, or some other exercise.

Before you can do that, however, you have to select a "starter" activity that makes sense for both of you and that helps you connect with your girl. That may take time and a little experimentation. But once you find the right activity—one that establishes a connection between you and your girl—get ready for a powerful connection.

When I worked at a youth support center for girls, one of my jobs was to add a greater physical dimension to the program as a whole. We started out by incorporating group hugs into the program—making them part of the routine at the beginning and end of our activities. The hugs had such a strong positive impact that I ended up asking one of my staff members, Vera, to "up the ante" by launching a weekly aerobics class. It started with a basic workout and got progressively more challenging as the weeks went by.

Without ever really meaning to, and without offering a word of advice on lifestyle issues, Vera developed some truly remarkable emotional connections between herself and the girls. The girls started volunteering important personal information during breaks in the workouts. As a group, they became supportive, enthusiastic, and (despite some impressive moaning and groaning about their exercise regimen) refreshingly optimistic. Mind you, they all complained about how much the workouts hurt—but they all kept showing up for the classes. Vera grew both personally and professionally as a result of the experience with "her girls." Miquela, one of her students, used the workout sessions to rediscover her own body, and boost her self-esteem, after having had two children. Miquela was only fourteen years old! Thanks to this and other work at the center, she re-entered school and got her life back on track. Vera was so proud of Miquela she that she almost couldn't speak. There were a dozen other girls with stories just as inspiring within that group.

That extraordinary network of connections and mutual reinforcements started modestly—with a series of hugs. It could have started with a collage, or with stitching, or with something else quite basic. For you and your girl, it can start with something as straightforward as a walk. But it *can't* start with advice.

Do What Works

If you don't like walking, consider a bike ride or any of a hundred other activities. The point is to get the heart beating and the blood pumping—not necessarily with the aim of developing an Olympic-level athlete, but in the hope of finding some pursuit that you and your girl can participate in comfortably and enthusiastically. The activity should help you share time together amiably. You want to find an activity that is its own conversation piece—or that will serve as a fit subject of attention when your girl decides that conversation is unnecessary for a few moments. That can be walking a dog—or going cross-country skiing—or practicing for a marathon. It all depends on where you and your girl are and what you like to do.

Remember: The act of using your body at the same time your girl is using her body allows for an "automatic focus" to the conversation. Physical action takes a great deal of pressure off both of you. When you or your girl can't think of anything to say, you don't have to say anything. You can keep stitching (or walking, or swimming, or jogging, or meandering through the amusement park) and still improve the quality and depth of your relationship.

Whatever activity you select, make sure it's something that you and your girl can enjoy together. This doesn't have to be the same activity you used to make initial contact with your girl. It does have to be something the two of you enjoy doing together. Beware! You're going to be working this activity into your girl's weekly schedule. It follows, then, that the activity should be something she likes doing—or at any rate likes doing with you. Don't fixate on an activity because *you* enjoy it. If the walk around the neighborhood bores your girl, try biking or swimming or some other activity that keeps both of you feeling alert and engaged.

The Next Step

You had a good outing or two—and your girl actually started to open up to you. What do you do next? Turn the physical activity into a regular event! Suggest that the two of you get together once or twice a week, at predetermined intervals, to spend time together and get a light workout.

This innocent-sounding suggestion will add structure and support to your girl's life. The vast majority of girls, I've found, will respond positively to such a suggestion. Just make sure not to let the girl know that you plan, in time, to increase the intensity and duration of your workouts. Be honest, but don't advertise your ultimate goal—a barrier-breaking commitment to shared physical exertion. For now, focus on how much fun it would be to get together on a regular basis—and keep the first few sessions comfortably within the "low-intensity buzz" category.

Some girls are extremely resistant to getting out and exercising. You're out to change that, of course, but you probably can't do it all at once. If you share your girl's resistance to the idea of regular exercise, let that be a strengthening of the bond between you—and make it clear that you're looking for support as you try to change your own pattern. If you can, enlist the aid of mutual friends or influential members of the girl's family. Do whatever you can to try to get her to make a commitment to a regular, prescheduled physical activity with you.

If you start hearing things like...

- "I don't like hiking"

- "I don't do that kind of stuff"

- "I don't like working out"

- "I don't feel like it"

then you might want to scale the activity back a bit. Suggest that you get together for a regular half-mile walk, rather than the full mile you did together last time. For now, the aim is to build a routine.

If you succeed in starting a mentor relationship with a girl, but find that she's resistant to further workouts, it may be because you're pushing too hard. You do want to raise the stakes, but you have to make the goals realistic. No, you can't do nail polish and magazines forever—but you shouldn't try to move from that phase to climbing Mt. Washington in a single day. This is an especially important point for mentors who already have a strong, established workout routine in their own lives. Help your girl build acceptance for the idea of a routine first.

Once she's used to—and enjoying—the practice of getting together with you on a regular basis, you'll find that the emotional connection between the two of you is quite strong indeed. You're ready to push your girl to move beyond her comfort zone with you.

Changing Behavior by Pushing the Limits

There's a pretty good chance that, from your previous experiences with this girl, you have a decent idea of what her tolerance level is. (Does she keep up with you during a

brisk walk—or huff and puff when you try to "air it out"?)
If you're uncertain about what she's capable of doing physically, ask around and find out. Ask the girl herself—see
how much information that yields. Then check with parents, friends, teachers, or whoever else seems to be in the
know. Find out if what you've got in mind in the "raising
the stakes" category is realistic. It's okay if what you're considering is outside of the girl's comfort level—in fact, it
probably should be—but it shouldn't be *too* far outside that
comfort level, at least not at first.

This "raising the stakes" strategy—challenging your girl
to move from magazine collages to walks in the park, from
walks in the park to hikes up a hill, and perhaps from hikes
up a hill to hikes up a mountain—serves a very important
purpose. You're going to challenge your girl—in a safe
environment, and in a completely supportive way. In other
words, you're going to get her used to the idea of undertaking challenges while she's with you, and you're going to use
physical activity as the backdrop for that experience.

It's vitally important that you subtly and supportively
raise the level of physical challenge within the relationship.
The aim here is simply to help her get used to the idea of
persistence. Climbing a higher mountain or biking a longer
route is important—but you have to keep the goals realistic
and accessible. Keep the physical activities fun and steadily
more challenging—by subtle gradations. In other words,
sneak in the increases in difficulty on your girl gradually—
don't drop them on her all at once.

Your girl has to learn how to press ahead even when times are tough, and she has to learn to draw on her own resources as she does so. Physical challenges—which can take the form of workouts, hikes, jogs, or camping trips—are great metaphors for real, live, grown-up existence because they usually feature at least one moment when your girl will say to herself, "Hey, I don't need this." But because you're there and she values her relationship with you, and because you'll be issuing all kinds of quiet encouragement, she'll learn to stick with it and keep working. And that's an essential survival skill in today's world if there ever was one.

I keep a motto pinned to my bulletin board, where the girls I mentor can see it.

KEEP ON
KEEP UP
KEEP AT IT

Even when times are hard, persistence is what pays off for grownups who have to make their way through a complicated, not always friendly world. That's a lesson girls need to learn first-hand from you. Boys tend to pick it up—in some form or another—with comparatively less trouble. For girls, serious goal orientation, and the sense of personal fulfillment that can come with it, are skills best achieved through physical activity with a mentor. My own experience is that there's really no better way to introduce the concept of persistence than to display it in some physical setting.

Is this an area where your own goals could use a little revision and expansion? Maybe you're not a physically active person. Maybe you've never really pushed yourself in this area. This is a great opportunity for you and your girl to grow at the very same time!

You've never tried rollerblading? Maybe it's time to learn—side by side with your girl. You'll fall down—but you'll laugh, too, and you'll have a great time encountering something entirely new. Perhaps most important, you'll serve as an example to someone who looks up to you—someone who's taken a hands-on attitude, avoided living life simply by rote, and taken a chance every once in a while. That's the way you want your girl to look at new challenges and new experiences. So show her. Do it yourself. Stretch yourself. Show her how to fall down—and get up with a smile on your face (or at least the kind of grimace that shows you take these things in stride). Be the model. Keep on getting up. Show her that there are times when you're not supposed to give up. Show her how the mind of a woman who's not about to surrender works.

You want to enact—not preach—some important lessons. Life is hard. You do fall down. You do have to decide to get back up.

Your girl doesn't need to *hear* about that. She needs to see it, and she needs to see it from you. Sometimes you'll take a spill; sometimes you'll get bruised. How will you respond to that? What message will you be sending your girl (and yourself)? It's not so much what happens that will make a big impression on your girl, but how you respond to what happens.

The big message you want to send through your "raising the stakes" campaign sounds something like this: "We're going to do something that will take some effort, and we might just fall down in the process. When that happens, we're going to get back up, brush ourselves off, and keep going, because you have to keep going when things don't go your way. Watch me. I'll show you how it works. You can do this."

It's nice to be able to support your girl with words like that. But, ultimately, you will have to let your own actions do the talking.

The Right Challenge Works Wonders

Some amazing things happen as a result of pushing girls to exert themselves physically. Once you've gone on two or three excursions with your girl, whether they're hikes, bike rides, trips to the gym, or other outings, you'll probably find that she'll be open to discussions of goal-setting and time management—or she may even bring up these topics herself. Just as Melanie brought up issues from her own past when we started working on the collage together, your girl may well initiate important conversations about "Where I'm going from here" or "How I can get to be like you?"

Once your girl trusts you and has experienced an appropriate physical challenge by your side, you'll find that lifetime habits of "shyness" or "awkwardness" may melt away when she's alone with you. Friendships with peers may have been difficult for your girl to manage at this stage in her life—but physical activities with you can bring on a sense of intimacy and involvement that makes setting up new relationships, or managing existing ones, quite a bit easier. Or perhaps a girl is having trouble managing her workload at school—particularly in areas such as mathematics, where girls may, as a statistical group, need more support to achieve at higher levels than boys. Physical activities with a mentor can make that challenge seem less intimidating. I've seen dramatic academic turnarounds happen time and time again as a direct result of carefully selected, consistently supported physical workout goals. This takes place all the time—and not necessarily because the mentor has (for instance) superior math skills and is willing to share them. That's certainly nice when it happens, but the real reason girls who experience barrier-breaking physical workouts often start performing better in school is that they have become accustomed to intense levels of emotional support that convince them they're capable of setting and attaining important goals in their own lives.

The truth is, there are dozens of areas where girls can benefit from the bonding, the emotional closeness, and the enhanced sense of self that arises from physical activity undertaken with a mentor. Whether they're...

- feeling more introspective

- struggling with feelings of inadequacy

- coming to terms with weight issues

- handling difficult changes at home

- working out the role a boyfriend will (or won't) play in their lives

- making sense of their own hormonal changes or the onset of menstruation

- grappling with major questions of identity or self-worth

... a set of regular physical workouts with a mentor will help girls make it through. These activities add challenge, accomplishment, and self-confidence on a very basic level and make it possible for girls to address even intense changes in their lives from a position of strength, with greater perspective and with increasing maturity.

Showing Vulnerability

When painful or confusing feelings surface in a girl's life—and rest assured that they will—that's a great time for you to offer up your own experiences of vulnerability and change. But don't do it in the abstract. Engage yourself in an activity that proves to the girl that she can "do it," too—by following your example and taking on something that seems scary or even impossible.

For instance, let's assume neither you nor your girl have ever gone rock climbing. Go sign up for a half-hour session at an indoor rock-climbing facility. Make sure your girl comes along with you. Let her see your initial feeling of uneasiness or discomfort—but also let her see your commitment to overcome the struggle and take on an exciting, and somewhat intimidating, new experience.

The lesson you're trying to pass along here is not that you're the kind of person who always shines, no matter what the challenge is. The message is that you're willing to take on the unknown, and that you're willing to support your girl as she tries, too.

Nobody succeeds every time. But we do have to give our best effort when we face a new and potentially intimidating experience. When you head up the face of that artificial rock, you're sending a powerful silent message. In essence, you're saying, "The outcome isn't ours to control— but the experience of doing something new *is* ours, and we can always use that experience to grow."

It's vitally important that we share our vulnerability in these situations, that we use physical activities as opportunities to demonstrate to girls that uncertainty really is a part of life. Our girls can and must learn how to handle uncertainty by following our example. Simply racing up the face of the rock isn't the point. You need to pick something that gives you a little wobble in your stomach, one that's roughly equivalent to the wobble your girl faces on a day-to-day basis in all those shifting, changing areas of her life. And you have to show her that, even though you're not familiar with the challenge that's in front of you right now, you're not going to opt out of the situation. You're going to give it your full attention and figure out how to make sense of what's in front of you.

Maybe you'll eventually become a world-class rock climber, and maybe you won't. But whether you do or not, you're going to figure out the best way to tackle this new challenge by translating your fear and uncertainty into the energy you need—and then tackling your goal.

Actually showing your girl how to harness uncertainty—the same process you'd use to tackle a difficult new project, or ask for a raise, or handle a challenge in your personal life—is possible in the context of a physical activity. And showing her is much, much more effective than lecturing her.

Undertake some physical challenge—choose it carefully, making sure to take into account your own and your girl's limitations and physical strengths. Propose customized challenges that make sense for her, where she is now—and make sure that the challenge you select for yourself is a boundary-pusher as well. Always look for ways to strengthen weaknesses and reinforce existing strengths.

Twenty Physical Activities You Can Share with Your Girl

1. Take an aerobics class.
2. Learn Tai Chi.
3. Take a country-music line dancing (or hip-hop) course.
4. Go skiing.
5. Take ice skating lessons.
6. Enter a walk-a-thon and raise dollars together.
7. Learn karate or judo for self-protection.
8. Join a nature hiking club.
9. Go canoeing.
10. Go whitewater rafting or kayaking.

11. Go camping with a women's group.

12. Take up rock climbing (indoor or outdoor).

13. Take a tennis class together.

14. Go golfing. (This can be a major networking opportunity.)

15. Take swimming lessons.

16. Go sledding in the winter.

17. Try body surfing.

18. Attend a gymnastics class or learn to work out on a trampoline.

19. Enroll in a weight training class.

20. Walk in your neighborhood on a regular basis—and, during every walk, learn three things neither of you knew before.

"I Can't"

It takes a little practice to know when—and how—to keep challenging your girl physically. For one thing, of course, you must always be careful to select a course of exercise that makes sense to both the girl and her parents. You may want to talk to a doctor about the appropriateness of a given activity. But once you find a physical challenge that makes sense for both of you and captures your girl's interest, you have to find a way to get her to move past her existing boundaries.

If you're out on a bike ride together, and your girl stops the bike and says she can't go on one more minute, be supportive and appropriately pushy. Realize that the goal of your time together is to get your girl to learn to push herself just a little beyond her comfort zone, and accept that, at least in the early going, you're going to have to do some of that pushing. Don't drive her to the edge of physical collapse, but do make sure she goes beyond her habitual level of performance. Chime in with something like: "Hey, I'm tired too, but I know you can do it. Come on. Just from here to that streetlamp up there, then we'll take a break. We'll do it together. Ready? Come on! One, two, three, together, and one, two, three, together, and one, two, three, together."

Don't encourage her to hurt herself. Encourage her to dig down deep within herself.

After you get off your bikes, and you're both panting in exhaustion, you can expect your girl to start whining, or even to be a little angry. She may...

- Swear that she'll never try anything like this with you again

- Demand that you explain why you did that to her

- Accuse you of pretending to enjoy what you just did

- Complain that you made her do something she didn't want to do

- Say you were too rough on her

- Express wonder that you or anyone could actually enjoy doing what you just did together

- Predict how sore she's going to be in the morning

- Ask you to promise you'll never do that to her again

Smile and take it all in stride. Use the moment as an opportunity to get closer to one another. Say (in your own words, of course), "Sure—it was difficult. It hurt. It hurts me, too. We're probably both going to be sore tomorrow. But we did it. You did it. And that's the most important thing. I knew you could do it. And I was right."

Words like those will almost certainly bring about a pause in the complaining. Enjoy that moment together. (And catch your breath!)

When you're certain she's registered the fact that she's transcended one of her own self-imposed boundaries, ask her a question: "What made you keep on going?"

She'll probably respond by saying something like, "Well, you made me do it."

Shake your head and set her straight. Let her know the power is hers, not yours. Say, "I didn't make you do anything. Nobody can make you do anything. You chose to do it. I encouraged you, but that's very different. You're the one who did the pedaling. You're the one who completed that course. You're the one who moved to the next level. You're the one who kept on going. So why did you keep on?"

She'll probably shrug her shoulders—or perhaps offer an answer that puts you in the middle of things again. That's when you should take the opportunity to remind her that the reason to keep going is to encourage belief in oneself—and that you saw a spark of that belief as she pushed herself to the very limit.

Tough Cases

What happens when you're working out with a girl who (assuming you're biking somewhere) throws the bike down and simply refuses to pedal another yard with you?

Every once in a while, of course, you find yourself face to face with a girl whose patience is short and who steadfastly refuses to have anything to do with even a modest physical challenge. This girl may say things like...

- "That's it."

- "I'm finished."

- "I'm not moving another muscle."

- "Forget it."

- "I told you, I can't do it."

And with that, she throws the bike down, sits on the side of the road, and pouts. She's angry. She's upset. She's humiliated. What do you do then?

What you do is put your own bike down and join her where she's sitting. You're going to show that you're willing to sit with this person, even when she's at her worst, and not lecture. After the blowup, don't offer suggestions, or goals, or encouragement, or anything else. Don't talk at all, not right now. Just allow her to feel the frustration, the anger. Allow her to take a rest while you sit together. Think of the prolonged silence I worked through with Melanie, and let that be your model. If I can survive that, you can sit with your girl through this sulk.

As you're doing so, take a moment to evaluate the situation: Did you ask too much of her? Did you set time limits that weren't appropriate? Was the target you set too ambitious? Is she really exhausted? Can you walk together for a while, or simply take an extended break of some kind? How far is it to the spot where you hoped to end your trip?

The main goal, though, is simply to let her understand that times do get rough in life, that this is one of those times, and that you're willing to be with her as it passes. After a few minutes, once she's moved past that point of anger and gotten some of the frustration out of her system, point out that you have faith in her. Explain to her how important it is for people to believe in themselves if they're going to attain important goals. And let her know that you know she's the kind of person who can pick herself up, dust herself off, and keep going—even if that means walking the bikes together for a while.

Let her know that you understand how frustrating things can be—and that there are times when people just have to be quiet. Make it clear that you're willing to share those times with her, too. Then, when things have calmed down a little—perhaps as you're concluding your session together that day—ask her where she wants to go from here and what kind of exercise regimen she thinks makes sense. Keep pushing—supportively—for a commitment to keep trying.

The "blowup" may be part of your relationship with your girl. All it really means is that you're pushing your girl a little harder than she's been pushed before. That's fine. As long as you're responsible in the goals you set, attentive to your girl's physical limitations, careful not to turn the physical challenge into an ego-driven game, and supportive of the emotions your girl feels as she learns to rely on herself, you can be sure you're doing the right thing.

Pushing Pays Off

The act of pushing your girl to "dig down deep" and attain some physically-oriented goal is not always easy for a mentor. It takes tact, solid instincts, and a willingness to take some emotional risks yourself. But it is certainly worth the trouble.

I've had girls give me the dirtiest looks during this phase of the relationship! And I've also had them come back to me after two weeks, or a month, or a year, and say, "You know, I really hated you that afternoon we went bike riding, it was the hardest thing. But you know what? It was a real turning point for me. You helped me a lot. You taught me how to get the most from myself. You helped me develop my ability to a point where I really didn't know I could perform." And there are some girls (often, I've found, those who blow up, toss down bikes, stalk away from the activity, etc.) who won't say that to their mentor's face, but who will say it to other people in their circle. Over the years, I've gotten plenty of evidence "through the grapevine" that physical challenges work—more than enough evidence to counterbalance the occasional blowups that have come my way.

Challenge Courses

After you've established the workout routine—after you've shared some strenuous physical activity two or three times—after your girl has gotten sore, gotten better, and realized that the world really doesn't come to an end once she pushes herself physically—then you're ready to launch the nastiest "trick" of them all: the challenge course.

The aim here is to help your girl create a deeper, more instinctive understanding of issues like planning, goal orientation, time management, and personal effectiveness. And you're going to use the same basic tool we've been examining throughout this chapter—physical activity—to do it.

Let's say the two of you have now biked two miles. You started out with one and a half miles, then the next week you came back and went for two. That last half mile of the two-mile course was a killer—but you did it. Maybe you pulled this off by turning the workout into a game, challenging each other, saying, "I know we can at least make it around that bend." And then when you made it around that bend, the end of your course was actually in sight, so you decided to keep on plugging and wrap up the two-mile course, since you were so close. It was a chore, but together, somehow, you pulled it off.

That's exactly what you're going to do now, but you're going to focus on a longer-term goal, a more distant "round the bend" goal.

Assume it's May, and you've just wrapped up that tough two-mile course. At some point, you're going to sit down with your girl and say, "Hey, why don't we set a goal for our-selves. Why don't we try to work our way up to three miles by November first. The two of us together—we'll plan it, and we'll work at it. We won't try to do it all at once, but we'll sort of edge our way up it, one ride at a time. What do you say?"

Of course, your goal doesn't have to have anything at all to do with bicycling a three-mile course. Perhaps it's get-ting through a ninety-minute aerobics class together at full force. Or experiencing a one-hour workout in seven differ-ent sports together. Or taking on a particularly challenging hike. Whatever the goal you come up with, it has to make sense to you—and to your girl—and it has to require sus-tained work over a protracted period. It's important for her to learn how to take care of her body now and long-term; steadily increasing exercise is a part of that. (For that matter, it's not a bad idea for most *mentors* to reinforce an appropri-ate long-term escalating exercise routine, either.) So take this opportunity to set a long-term physical goal that the two of you can pursue together.

You're out to get more than a workout, though. Your aim is to create the experience of moving toward a distant goal—not simply working out or going out on a hike for the fun of it, but actually striving to attain something impressive in the long term. You're out to prove that that can be inspiring and enjoyable and empowering—in addition to being (occasionally) frustrating and painful.

In other words, you're not just showing up for aerobics—you're making a tangible difference in two lives, yours and your girl's. You're out to prove that you're both willing to stick to the work necessary to turn a major long-term goal into a reality.

The Power of Two

Part of the power of the challenge course arises from the sense of partnership it entails. Committing yourself to a goal only you know about sometimes means you have a moment of passion for that goal. Committing yourself to a goal that someone else knows about, and is working toward with you, means you have a series of moments of passion for that goal. You and your partner support one another consistently as you work toward the goal. Developing lists of mutual goals also means that people can't back away from their own goals as easily, which is a benefit mentors shouldn't underestimate if they're trying, for instance, to lose a few stubborn pounds!

You can and should put this basic "talk about it" principle—which I call the "power of two"—to work for yourself and your girl.

If you're having trouble getting your girl to commit to a sensible challenge course, that is, one that makes sense to you, the girl's parents, and a physician—there's another idea you can use to build up trust and increase the likelihood that your girl will change her mind. This strategy picks up on the idea of sharing moments of vulnerability with your girl; it can be quite effective. Ask her to accompany you on your annual physical exam, or (even better) ask for her help and support during medical procedures that you undergo that carry emotional implications. I'm thinking specifically of mammograms—bringing your girl along on these appointments is a great way to let her know that you trust her fully. Including her helps her learn to think long term, and shows her how you respond to an important responsibility that many women evade.

By accompanying you on one of your own medical visits, your girl will learn how essential it is to offer emotional support to a friend and ally. The shared experience will almost certainly strengthen the emerging bond between the two of you, and will encourage your girl to share important information with you about her own health and physical development. The visit will heighten the "power of two" phenomenon, leaving each of you feeling strongly committed to the other person's cause. If your girl won't commit to some kind of challenge course after sharing this experience with you, then she probably never will.

There's another important lesson your girl will learn by accompanying you on a visit to a doctor. As women, we are often inclined to take care of ourselves last. By taking care of everyone else first, we may put our own health and well being in jeopardy. That's not how we want any of our daughters to treat themselves. We want them to learn that they're responsible for tending to important issues of physical health, that there's no stigma in doing so, and that there's no advantage in postponing important questions that have to do with their own well-being. If you're a professional woman who's "too busy" to schedule yourself for a mammogram (or, for that matter, an annual physical examination), then there are two people whose behavior and references you need to change for the better: yourself and your girl! Take the opportunity to deepen this relationship and make a commitment to take care of yourself. If taking the time to make an appointment is difficult, share the challenge with your girl and talk with her about how you plan to overcome it.

After your experience, appeal to your girl once again about the challenge course you've discussed. She may well change her mind.

Working on a challenge course together means going past the comfort zone, time after time. It means yelling to your partner, "We can do it!" when you're both tired and sweaty and aching in every joint of your body, when it would be ever so much easier to stop short of your goal that day and go home. It means pressing the issue. And that means working with your girl on a regular basis to move past complacency and petrified ritual.

You may need to put out a fair amount of energy at first to wear down your girl's instinctive "Why bother?" response. Young girls—and, truth be told, our society as a whole—have become alarmingly resistant to the very idea of sustained, escalating physical challenge. I think many girls who resist challenge courses are only reflecting the role models they see around them day after day. The role models girls are exposed to, all too often, are people who watch way too much television and choose, for whatever reason, not to exercise consistently.

Getting excited about going past the comfort zone may not come instinctively to your girl. Even after she makes a commitment to you, she may need some help getting motivated about that commitment; she may need someone to remind her of that commitment and hold her to it. That's what you're there for: to get past that familiar "It's no big deal, why should I bother" facade, and to help your girl appreciate the exhilaration that comes with pressing up against the comfort zone over a period of time with someone you love and respect.

Unconditional Conditions

Remember: Regardless of how they may present themselves to you and to the world at large, girls are eager to spend time with an older woman who will share outlooks, experiences, and insights with them. You must be willing to do so—but you must also have an agenda.

Your supportiveness and your ability and willingness to listen must be unconditional, with a couple of unspoken conditions. You have to show an unstinting, but tactfully expressed, distaste for complacency in any facet of life, and especially for physical complacency. You're not going to talk your girl out of watching soap operas all day long ("I don't know why you waste your time on that stuff."). Instead, you're going to pleasantly pester your girl into taking physical action, again and again, until something interesting happens. ("What a beautiful day it is outside! You remember that run we were talking about last week? This would be the perfect day for it! Why don't you go put on some sweats? We can give it a go right now, and get back in time for [*All My Children* / time with friends at the mall / whatever.])

Complacency is the enemy of personal growth—in the physical realm and in any number of other realms, as well. That's the lesson you're trying to get across, not with words, but with deeds. That's a big part of what growth in life is: You've reached a certain level, and now it's time to go on to the next level, to find out something new and exciting about yourself and the world in which you live. The only way to do that is to move past your comfort zone, that spot that doesn't require much effort to maintain. You have to learn how to seek out that moment when your heart starts pounding and your adrenaline starts flowing and you start feeling those butterflies in your stomach. You have to seek out a certain amount of pain, physical and otherwise.

That's not masochism. That's a commitment to ongoing growth and development. That's a personal challenge course kicking in and getting ready to go to work. That's physical activity in and of itself—and physical activity as a metaphor for a larger, broader, and essential act of self-renewal. How does that old Bob Dylan song go? The one about the only person not being born is the one busy dying?

If the lesson could be well and truly learned by simply reading it, I'd be the first one to tell you that all you need to do is sit your girl down, show her this section of the book, and ask her to read over the key paragraphs a few times. Unfortunately, personal growth is not that easy. Your girl has to do more than know what we're talking about in this chapter. She has to feel it, and she has to feel it with you by her side.

When your girl feels a physical challenge in that way, when she makes a commitment to her own personal challenge course, she will start learning how to reflect it back to a hundred other situations in her life. She will start using the struggle for physical goals as an experience that can help her understand how she has to respond when she encounters other events in her life that make her feel like giving up. And these days, there's probably no shortage of those kinds of events.

After they've taken on a personal commitment to a challenge course, girls are able to reflect back on what they've learned from you and say, "I've done this before. I understand this feeling. I worked really hard to be able to know what to do when I run into this feeling. She trained me; she helped me understand what to do when I get into this situation. I can make it through this. I trust myself to do the right thing here."

Moving to the Next Level

Whatever you choose to do in the long term, do it together. Learn together. Grow together. And you'll become stronger— together.

The challenge course allows you to add a sense of purpose—shared purpose—to the activities you and your girl take on. In other words, you're not simply finding something new and exciting, something the two of you have never done. You're making a series of plans and choices with a long-range goal in mind. You're pointing yourself toward that goal for the express purpose of taking both yourself and your girl to the next level.

You're not just taking on a new experience for the thrill of it. You're doing some planning together. You're asking:

- What do we need to do to move to the next level by such-and-such a time?

- How are we going to organize our efforts to achieve this goal?

- What's going to have to happen between point A and point B?

- How are we going to get proficient enough over the next (week, month, two months) to make the attainment of that long-term goal realistic?

Once you and your girl are looking at a meaningful goal that can only be attained in the long term, you're both going to have to get together to sketch out exactly how that goal is going to come about. That means developing planning skills, and (probably just as important) accepting that a big dream doesn't take place overnight.

The challenge course is one of the very best ways to help your girl learn that important things happen, not by wishing or hoping, but as the result of someone sitting down, breaking the job up into smaller chunks, setting up a strategy—and then taking action. If you can use a regimen of physical activity to help your girl develop those habits, then you will have done her one of the biggest favors of her life.

Variations on the Challenge Course

Let's say the girl that you're working with lives on the other side of the country. Can you still find some way to incorporate a physical challenge into your exchanges—or even use it as the foundation for your relationship?

It's easier than you think. Find out what she's doing. Write her a letter. Send her an e-mail. Say, "I've started to do this one-mile bike ride every week, and I want to challenge myself to work it up to three miles by the first of November. It would be really great if I had your support on this, if I knew you were taking the same steps I'm taking right now. Can you take on this goal too? Can we keep in touch about how it's going—and perhaps even synchronize our schedules? Why don't we make an agreement that the two of us will challenge each other on this and check in by phone after each ride?"

This approach provides you with an opportunity to keep up-to-date with her on a weekly or monthly basis. You can either set up specific check-in times beforehand ("We'll talk every Saturday night about the ride we completed that day"), or take a more informal approach ("Hey, I just made it up to two miles today—how was your last ride?"). The challenge course allows her to have a reason to call you, too. Physical activity serves the same purpose when you and the girl are at a distance that it does when you're working side-by-side.

It gives you a subject to talk about comfortably and a set of shared experiences.

After you develop some proficiency working one-on-one with your girl, you may feel inspired to start challenge courses that involve groups. With my Girl Scout troop, I set up a relay race, marked by buckets filled with old clothes, that *turned into* a challenge course. The girls successfully completed the course I set for them—then they wanted to do it faster and faster and faster. They set targets for improvement, and we all worked together to do what was necessary to meet them. That race was a lot of fun: When the first girl reached the bucket, she had to put on, say, a big overcoat—and then race back, take off the overcoat and hand it to the next person in line. It got quite energetic, and the girls ended up being more ruthless than I would ever have dreamed of about improving their times!

Don't be surprised when the girl you're working with starts setting new goals for herself. That's what a challenge course can do—what it's meant to do—help your girl transfer your "You can do it!" into her own "I can do it!"

Communicating Becomes Easy, Planning Becomes Easy

When you use physical activity to initiate or deepen your relationship with a girl, you give her permission to express important questions and observations about physicality itself. Eventually, you can raise your own issues or present physical goal-setting in a way that doesn't seem threatening, intimidating, or overbearing. When you take part in enough physical activities with a girl, even with a girl who's on the other side of the continent, it soon becomes acceptable (and relatively easy!) to talk about...

- What your body looks and feels like

- What her body looks and feels like

- Where your energy level is

- Where her energy level is

- What you'd like your energy level to be

- What she'd like her energy level to be

- What physical changes you want to see in your life

- What physical changes she wants to see in her life

- Self-esteem and self-worth issues you've associated with your physicality

- Self-esteem and self-worth issues she's associated with her physicality

- Where you both want to go next

It may seem difficult, or even impossible, to address those issues in the abstract, with no physical context to allow shared experience and shared goal-setting. But *with* that context, and a willingness on your part to show some vulnerability first, I think you'll find that your girl will start opening up to you in some truly remarkable ways.

Sharing feelings and reactions is a major reason you're emphasizing physical activity in the first place, so don't skip that step. Build some "connection time" into your workout ritual. I know a gym teacher who uses her initial class time as an opportunity to connect with each and every one of the girls assigned to her. She takes the first few minutes just to talk about what's going on in her own life, where she's trying to make progress in terms of her own physical goals. She helps them see how a training calendar works, lets them take a look at what she herself has accomplished recently, and shows them what she's planned for the month to come. That's a dramatic, person-to-person way to make goal-setting a reality for the girls she's working with. They're not staring at a textbook; they're looking at what their instructor actually has planned for the next thirty days!

One of the very best ways to make workouts fun is to introduce new kinds of planning around physical experiences. Let your girl see how you plan these things and then encourage her to do the same. So pull out your Day Timer, your Palm Pilot, or the yellow legal pad that serves as your ongoing to-do list—and let her take a look.

The Benefits of the Physical Approach

By emphasizing physicality and moving toward challenge courses, you're helping your girl learn how to create healthy tension and excitement in her own life whenever she needs it. You're using physical activity to let her experience the excitement of starting a new race, a new hike, a new ride, one she's never completed before. You're helping her learn to conquer the same uneasiness and uncertainty that's likely to come her way when she has to make a presentation at work, launches a new product, takes on the training duties for an entire new division, or has to repair a complex piece of equipment. You're helping her learn to conquer fear.

You're helping her choose to be reborn, day after day, week after week, month after month—rather than give in or seek out a (seemingly) comfortable, withdrawn place when things get difficult.

The younger your girl is when she learns these all-important lessons, the better chance she'll have of rising to the challenges life throws her way. The younger she is when she learns what it's like to have to dig down deep to meet a physical challenge, the more likely she is to be able to benefit from that lesson instinctively as she grows.

To recap, the ideas in this chapter can be boiled down to two fundamental steps:

- Step one: Use some kind of physical activity—appropriate to the situation and the girl's personality and background—to support your efforts to reach out.

- Step two: Once you've developed a good relationship with the girl and gained an informed idea of what her limitations and abilities are, find an activity that pushes her beyond her comfort zone. Pester her supportively until she gives it her all. Eventually, you should establish a challenge course the two of you can carry out together.

If you carry out both of these steps, you'll have exerted a positive, constructive influence that will, quite literally, last a lifetime. At some level, when your girl becomes an adult and faces the inevitable challenges that await mature people who are committed to growth and development, she will hear your voice. She'll hear you exhorting her to reach down deep inside herself, and she'll remember how you helped her to overcome a seemingly impossible problem—by appealing to the best within herself, by taking specific steps toward a goal, and by using strength she didn't know she had to meet a new challenge.

All of which, of course, is a way of saying that she'll hear you, for years to come, insisting that she believe in herself. And, in her memory, she'll also see you believing in yourself as you rode the bike, climbed the hill, jogged that final mile, or hung in there through a tough workout. Those sounds and images will stay with her, and inspire her, again and again, to go to her own next level.

What's the Alternative?

Not long ago, I was on a talk show with a young girl who had some serious self-image problems. She had been experimenting sexually—and had had intercourse with several boys—but the experiences had not left her feeling happier or more self-confident, as she'd imagined they would. Here she was, feeling as though she was simply giving her body away to any and every male who expressed an interest in her—on the theory that doing so would somehow improve her self-image. In fact, she felt more and more valueless.

She was tall and willowy and beautiful. It was easy to see why she was turning as many heads as she was. But all her beauty and her seductiveness had provided her with was a profound feeling of having been used by every sexual partner she had ever chosen. She asked me lots of questions, both on and off camera. In essence, she wanted to know, "How do I change? How do I overcome these feelings of not being worthwhile?" I told her that sex (or the promise of sex) was not the measure of her worth as a person. She nodded, but I realized that no simple sentence or two from me would answer her unspoken underlying question: "What do I *replace* sex with? How do I get the same feeling of belonging, of acceptance, of exhilaration—and make it last?"

The most painful part of this story is that this girl was only fourteen years old. Like so many girls in her situation, she looked a good deal older. My heart nearly broke when I realized what she was up against.

It so happened that she lived in the state of Washington—one of the most beautiful regions in the entire country, with mountain ranges that leave you breathless, whether you climb them or simply stand in awe in front of them. I say that as someone who loves my own home state of New York, but who has been lucky enough to visit the Pacific Northwest. If you've never hiked, biked, climbed or kayaked in rural Washington, you've missed one of life's great outdoor experiences.

It was clear to me that this girl didn't need another lecture about how it was wrong of her to go to bed with boys who found her attractive, and whom she found attractive. I could tell, just from a few moments of listening to her, that she'd had plenty of such lectures in the past, and that, however well intentioned they may have been, those sermons had had little positive effect. She was in a critical period of her life, a period of turmoil and doubt and pain, a period when questions of self-definition were taking on immense importance. She was in search of peak experiences, experiences that would help her to come up with an answer when she found herself looking at herself in the mirror each evening and wondering who was staring back.

The way to help her make sense of the difficult life situation she faced, I realized, was not to make her feel bad about what she'd already done—that would only lower her self-image further, and, in all likelihood, encourage her to seek out emotional support in exactly the same way she'd been doing. No, the way to help this girl to point her life in a new direction was for someone mature, someone who had no sexual interest in her whatsoever, to reach out and say, "Come on—let's go take a walk in the mountains together."

Talk about a sensual experience! Talk about a life-defining encounter! With a mentor at her side, hiking through that exquisite countryside, she'd be able to explore the limits of her body, reinforce her sense of self, and, perhaps, by making her way up one of those eye-popping summits, push herself just a little further than she'd ever been able to push herself before. She'd feel more connected with her body, with her emerging physical power, with the security of a relationship with someone whom she could trust, than she would in twenty afternoon encounters with boys after school. (If nothing else, a thoughtful mentor who made such a "come-on" to her would give her something to do in the hours between three and five, when a good percentage of teen sex takes place.)

She'd learn to develop love for herself as she moved her muscles and pushed her system to its limit. She'd focus her energies in a way that supported her—instead of moving her muscles in a way that means giving away her body to the next boy (or man!) with a well-practiced "sales pitch."

She was a fourteen-year-old girl with a beautiful physique. I realized that she should be putting that body through a challenge course, one that would enable its owner to see how much she was capable of doing, how disastrous the prolonged neglect and sabotage of her own powers and capabilities would be, and how much was to be gained by following the example of an older woman. She needed a different kind of "physical mentor"—one who knew what it takes to manage the transition from child to adult, one who wouldn't take advantage of her, one who wouldn't let her succumb to the fear inherent in the words "I can't."

Needless to say, that show was a very emotional experience for me. Before we parted, I got her name and address and made a commitment to myself to track down someone in the Washington area who'd be able to launch those hiking expeditions—or find a way to do it myself.

There are millions of girls like her. They can be found in virtually every city, town, and suburb of our society.

Peak Experiences

We have to be there for girls like the one I met on that talk show, girls who are desperate to find out who they are and need only the right channels to learn that the answer lies within themselves. We have to show them how much is possible for them by taking the natural drives that God has instilled in their bodies—and by using those drives in constructive, self-supporting ways.

We can't hold back the lessons that nonsexual physical "peak experiences" have to offer them. We must help them experience their bodies in a way that says, "You're blessed. God has given you legs and arms that move, lungs that breathe, a heart that beats, a mind that reels in joy when you push yourself to the limit. You're truly blessed. Don't hide from this power you feel, don't pretend it doesn't exist, don't listen to anyone who tells you that the power of your body is evil. It's not evil. It's your treasure. And you're important enough to use the power you feel in a way that supports you. That's part of the blessing God has given you with this body—the ability to use its energies in ways that make you feel good about yourself, rather than bad about yourself."

That's not the whole message, though. By using physical activities to reach out to girls like the one I met in that television studio, and by sharing challenge courses with them, we ourselves are blessed. When we help a girl learn, first-hand, how to live life constructively, we reinforce every good choice we ourselves have ever made in our own lives. We become better friends, better lovers, better mates, better mothers, better at everything. We do the work we were meant to do; we help make mature, supported growth the reality that women are meant to share with one another.

That physical awakening is meant to be passed along from the older to the younger, from the experienced to the inexperienced, from the seasoned to the virginal. When we share our bodies with these girls, we capture a part of that youthful spark, that dynamic edge, that fresh exuberance that women-to-be and only women-to-be can bring to life. I believe, based on my own experience, that sharing a positive, nonsexual, boundary-smashing physical challenge with a girl or a young woman comes powerfully close to sharing in that which is truly liberating and, yes, holy, in day-to-day life.

Reaping the Rewards

Many of the adult women who come to my seminars are intimidated by the seemingly daunting task of making a physical commitment to a challenge course with their girls. Those who actually make the leap and push both themselves and the girls who need them to reach a little further than ever before, unanimously report that the rewards both mentors and girls experience far exceed the investment of time and energy.

So my challenge to you is simple: Accept that, once you've made a commitment to make a positive change in a girl's life, you have, by definition, made a commitment to reach out to her by means of physical activity. You must then nag, cajole, drop hints, and show up on the doorstep in your workout gear until that girl sets out on a challenge course with you. Once you see the initial commitment through, I promise you you'll be convinced, before too long, that you've made the right choice—the only sensible choice—for all our daughters.

5

The Second Essential: Intellectual Development

Whether your girl is a straight-A student, is struggling with her studies, or falls somewhere in between those two poles, she needs the opportunity to learn and to be challenged intellectually. What's more, she has a right to enjoy intellectual challenges, and mentors have an obligation to help make that enjoyment a reality.

Intellectual growth and development is not an option that some gifted girls may, if they're lucky, find themselves in a position to take advantage of. It's a necessity. If the opportunity to expand her intellectual horizons is held back from your girl, or if there's no one to push her to develop her "learning" muscle in new and exciting ways, then she'll be disadvantaged in a way she shouldn't. Her ability to adapt to new and challenging circumstances—her ability to rise to the occasion when presented with something that's not familiar to her—will suffer, perhaps irreparably.

Note that here I'm not talking about helping your girl cram massive amounts of "content" into her brain so that she can regurgitate it onto a test form and never encounter the information again. What I'm talking about is the process of getting comfortable with learning itself—the phenomenon that allows mature, healthy, intellectually curious people to look at a new set of challenges and say, "Hey, what if..." rather than, "Gee, beats me."

Yvonne's Story

Yvonne's father died when she was twelve. Her father had had an immense impact on her intellectual life—he was a dedicated visitor of museums and had instilled a love of reading in Yvonne. Although Yvonne was a bright and inquisitive child—thanks largely to her father's influence— the loss had been a crushing blow to her, and as she stood on the verge of her teen years, Yvonne began to withdraw, both socially and academically. The change was a painful and ironic one for the people who loved Yvonne. Her father had, after all, been a high school principal—and now she was having trouble in school.

Yvonne's aunt, Vera, looked long and hard at the situation her favorite niece faced—and decided to take action. Vera started thinking about what Yvonne's father would have done had he lived, and about the kinds of steps he would have taken to keep his daughter alert, engaged, and curious about the world around her. After a long period of thought and prayer, Vera nominated herself as Yvonne's mentor, and made a

commitment to help support Yvonne's intellectual development in the coming years.

Each year, she and Yvonne planned a special "excursion
week" together—a journey to a new spot, someplace
Yvonne had never been before. (Yvonne's Uncle Frank also
helped in the planning and accompanied them on the trip.)
Those trips were special times—and they were something
Yvonne could count on during a particularly important
period in her life. The three visited all kinds of spots in the
U.S., and even made a visit to Europe while Yvonne was in
high school, thanks to a year of penny-pinching. During one
of the trips—that week-long journey to Paris when Yvonne
was fifteen—Vera and Yvonne started talking about Yvonne's
educational goals. Vera learned that Yvonne had long desired
to become a lawyer, but now felt that her family's financial
situation, which had often been difficult after her father's
death, made such a goal all but impossible. Even college
seemed unaffordable.

During that memorable trip to Paris, Vera told Yvonne
something that had an extraordinary impact on her later in
life. She convinced her niece that if her grades were good
enough, and if she found ways to participate in student government and sports activities—if, in short, she became a
model student—she could win a full scholarship to college
and be in a good position to attain her long-term goal of
becoming a lawyer.

Yvonne accepted that strategy, and when the time came
to apply for college, she wrote her admission essay about
the extraordinary care, commitment, and love her aunt had

shown her in arranging her yearly trips. Yvonne wrote in glowing detail of all she had learned during her "excursion week" trips—the people she had met, the new cultures she had encountered, the ideas she had been exposed to. She spent a lot of her essay talking about what she had learned about France during the week she'd spent there.

That essay, combined with Yvonne's superior grades and heavy participation in school government and sports activities, won her a full scholarship at a prestigious women's college. Today, she's well on her way to attaining that law degree. And it all started because a mentor was willing to expose her to new cultures, new locations, and new experiences—and challenge her at a key point in her development.

Yvonne's story has a happy ending—or a happy beginning, depending on how you look at it—but that outcome required lots of hard work from a woman who loved her and was willing to reach out to her and support her intellectual growth. Countless girls just like Yvonne need that kind of support, and when they don't receive it, they fall prey to big problems.

Structural Challenges: The "Academic Falloff"

Many girls who have done very well in grade school and middle school, but who lack an effective support network (such as the one Yvonne had) embark on a pattern of mediocre or substandard performance once they enter high school or junior high school. Why does this happen?

Why do a large number of girls—perhaps the majority— suddenly become content with distinctly modest achievements in school? Why, when girls enter junior high school and high school, do their levels of self-esteem seem to plummet? Why do these girls no longer participate as aggressively in math and science courses? Why are many high school and junior high school girls far less likely to take risks or assert themselves in class than they were only a few years before?

The answers to these questions are complex, and I could probably fill a book this size if I attempted to address the issue in as much detail as it deserves. Some of the "academic falloff" phenomenon among girls appears to be traceable to social and gender dynamics operating within the classroom, shifts that may have both social and biological influences. For many girls, the emphasis during these years turns away from schoolwork and toward dating and interacting with boys. For reasons that may not yet be fully understood, many girls also face a "built-in" decrease in academic support and motivation as they move into their junior high school and high school years. That is to say, even the most well-intentioned female teachers often have a habit of calling on junior high and high school age boys—who tend to be far more aggressive and forthcoming than girls of the same age—with much greater frequency than they call on the girls in the same class.

Much in modern print and broadcast media exacerbates the "academic falloff" phenomenon among girls and young women during these years. Media appeals win attention—and dollars—from girls via highly manipulative messages, especially those contained in advertising campaigns. Today's short-term, bottom-line driven media, where audience totals are everything, are often much better at exacerbating the problems contributing to girls' academic obstacles than proposing possible solutions. Countless advertisements, videos, and popular magazine articles encourage girls to focus on boys, fashion, and sex to the exclusion of virtually any other topics. That these appeals are effective is hard to deny. That they support healthy personal development in their target audience, or are in the least concerned about any long-term responsibility to that audience, is impossible to believe.

Girls who watch MTV regularly—and millions do—are bombarded with messages that say, in essence, that one's life is and ought to be dependent on getting hormones to kick in, hormones that are quite capable of kicking in on their own. The result is a perpetuation of the complex (and already powerful) social values that encourage girls to withdraw from personal routines that support academic achievement during adolescence.

Encouraging girls and young women to define their self-worth according to the approval or disapproval they receive from males is a potentially catastrophic game—and although it may work well as a marketing plan, it can have powerful negative effects on the lives of the girls who fall prey to that plan. Until the day when boys begin defining themselves exclusively as companions for girls, with support of the media, girls will need special attention and emphasis when it comes to developing the self-esteem and coping strategies that foster healthy intellectual development. Girls need to receive other messages, healthier messages, than the ones they receive from billboards, television, and magazines—and the mentors in their lives have to help send those messages.

A Living Example

Your goal as a mentor is not to redesign the public school system or boycott the media outlets that (intentionally or otherwise) encourage girls to withdraw on the academic level. Your goal is much more practical. You have to provide perspective and help to fill the gaps. You have to help your girl come in contact with exciting new worlds that extend beyond the classroom, lest she come to believe the fatal myth that all human learning takes place while one is staring at a blackboard. (You'll be learning about some effective strategies for getting that message across later on in this chapter.) And, just as important, you'll need to serve as a model of sane behavior and perspective in your dealings with others. Simply through your continued presence in your girl's life, and your ability to help her encounter new intellectual challenges, you'll be sending some powerful (and usually unspoken) messages: As important as it may seem at times, finding a man to be with is not the only worthwhile personal and intellectual goal. Life is full of change, opportunity, and excitement, and exposure to it is stimulating and healthy. And while they may love and respect the man in their life—if they have one—strong women are quite capable of exploring new environments and overcoming obstacles without the guidance of that man.

As a mentor, you have to be willing to show (rather than tell) your girls that you believe in these principles and make important, exciting life choices based on them. After all, the odds are that we will outlive the men in our lives, and a good portion of us will divorce at least one!

Help your girl prepare for the challenges she's going to face. Be ready to fill in the gaps left by school systems and advertising-driven media machines. Be ready to help her achieve her full potential intellectually. Let her see that you're perfectly capable of exploring new situations on your own, and that she can do the same.

In this chapter, you'll learn some strategies for helping your girl develop a love of new environments and new experiences during her junior high school and high school years—and beyond. In doing so, you will augment, not replace, the education she receives in the classroom. You'll help make learning real and tangible. And you'll make it more likely that she'll emerge from her adolescence as a healthy, well-rounded, self-sufficient individual.

Customizing Your Approach

Of course, different girls need different kinds of academic and intellectual support. One of the things mentoring can always do, however, is encourage the sense of discovery and wonder that leads to the exploration of new intellectual worlds—the vast, exciting horizons of knowledge that await discovery in the arts and sciences.

By finding out what excites and motivates your girl, you can learn what you need to about the best way to reach out to her on an intellectual level. Every girl will be different—but every girl will respond to something. By finding out what already "jazzes" their girls, and working from there, mentors can take a good deal of the stigma of boredom away from the act of "studying." They can help to make "studying" less of a passive, receptive activity and help turn it into an active, engaged, hooked-in examination of how what's going on in the world now actually affects your girl's daily life.

Connections

If you're looking for the simplest way to make a big difference in your girl's intellectual development, here it is: Introduce her to the intelligent women in your own personal network.

It's particularly inspiring for girls to meet women in different disciplines who've put training and intellectual firepower to practical use in their own lives. Whether you provide that exposure yourself, or you serve as a conduit who allows your girl to meet a female scientist, scholar, artist, entrepreneur, or activist, you should consider taking advantage of an opportunity to help your girl reach out to someone. Help her come in contact with a woman who can demonstrate precisely why—and how—knowledge can translate into autonomy and power in a woman's life.

You might decide to...

- Take your girl to lunch with your boss.

- Bring your girl to a seminar at which a female motivational speaker is appearing.

- Invite your girl to go jogging or work out with a colleague you respect.

- Introduce your girl to a woman who represents an important client or vendor who works with your business.

- Ask your girl to join you in attending a networking event sponsored by a female leadership organization (such as the American Association of University Women [202-785-7700], or the National Association of Women Business Owners [800-266-8762]).

- Go with your girl as she visits her mother on the job.

That last item can be a particularly powerful experience for your girl. She may be used to seeing her mother exclusively in a domestic setting; she may not think of her mother as a person who makes decisions, balances budgets, deals with crises, or has to come up with a solution when other people don't follow through on commitments. If your girl's mother has a career outside the home, don't make everyone wait until Take Our Daughters to Work ® Day. Help your girl learn more about her mother's identity and coping strategies as a working person. Arrange a mutually convenient time for her to watch her mother in action.

Beyond the Classroom

Many effective strategies for broadening your girl's intellectual horizons will involve going somewhere with your girl.

Get out and about. Move beyond the classroom or anything that looks like it. Leave that terrain to your girl's teacher. Show your girl where *else* people learn about things. Stimulate her by changing her surroundings, or, at the very least, getting her to associate learning with someplace that is new and exciting.

Whether you're in a suburb, a small town, or a large city, you'll want to make a trip that will directly involve yourself—and your girl—in some discipline that can make a difference to her. Your role is to help encourage your girl to explore the many people, places, and opportunities that await her outside of the formal boundaries of the classroom. That means shared expeditions undertaken side by side. These trips represent a way for both of you to explore the outside world in an exciting, engaging way—and for getting the idea across that learning means exploring.

Ideally, your travels should be guided by your girl's interests and convictions, but in the very early stages of the relationship, you may not know enough about your girl to select a destination that's perfectly targeted. Pick one that's *imperfectly* targeted, but still likely to get her to open up to you and talk about what she likes and doesn't like. Good, low-risk first-time journeys for the girl you're trying to help could include:

- The state capitol building or City Hall. (Guided tours of historic buildings open up all kinds of avenues for discussion.)

- A theater or dance presentation. (Perhaps you can explore both a community theater production and a first-rate show from a top local theater or troupe—and then talk about the difference between the two productions.)

- The office of a local female legislator or other elected official. (If you live near Washington, D.C., you can try to combine a monument-hopping trip with a prearranged visit with a woman who serves your town, city, or community in some capacity.)

- A major local museum. (These are great initial outings for virtually all girls and represent classic initial outings that can help expose your girl to new possibilities at virtually no cost.)

- A nearby major national park. (Ask for all the information you can find on when and why the park was selected.)

- A local tourist attraction you and your girl have not yet visited. (This can be especially important if your girl is a resident of an inner-city neighborhood—she needs to learn that the commercial sectors of the city, the spots where the crowds and glamour and excitement are, are meant for her as well. She is a resident of the city, with every right to enjoy its resources, famous or otherwise. Help her experience that which is popular—but not yet familiar through direct interaction—by means of a day trip or bus tour.)

- Any other exciting part of the city in which your girl lives with which she's unfamiliar. (Don't let her buy into artificial limitations about where she can and can't go!)

A Sense of Belonging

Sometimes, girls stop growing intellectually—and on other fronts—because they feel deeply threatened by the environments in which they live. The mentor's job in this situation is to arrange for exposure to new and stimulating circumstances, and fast. In most cases, you'll want to take a trip together to help her cultivate a sense of belonging—but this "journey" doesn't always have to take the form of a trip to a new physical locale.

There's a girl I know—I'll call her Antonia—whose family moved to the suburbs a while back. She's fifteen years of age, and she grew up in the city. While she was living in the city, she spent most of her time hanging out with her group of school friends. Once she made it out to the suburbs, she felt quite isolated and alone.

When I met her, Antonia had lived in her new home for a year and a half, but she still hadn't been able to develop a new group of friends. She didn't seem to fit in anywhere. The more isolated she felt, the more she acted out in ways that made her mom worry about her, and the worse her grades got. It was as though this girl hadn't completely developed a way of living that worked for her in the suburbs. She was used to the hustle and bustle of the city and the easy access to places and events that would stimulate her.

Antonia and I had the chance to talk together, and I asked her about the things that excited her and made her feel good. It turned out that she had a deep interest in learning more about her own Hispanic culture—and particularly about Hispanic women. But how was she supposed to find out about them—outside of the confines of her (supposedly) "boring" school library? I took the opportunity to introduce her to the World Wide Web, and we did some browsing together at my house.

I was able to point her to different sites that introduced her to a huge number of high-achieving Hispanic women in history—some of whom were running their own successful businesses. In just a few days she was an expert Internet surfer. She's now begun a dialogue with some successful female entrepreneurs who've served as effective "virtual" mentors for her. Her performance at school—and her relationship with her mother—have improved dramatically.

The experience was a powerful and positive one for Antonia. Before she and I sat down together at the terminal, she really didn't know how big the world out there was; she didn't know that there were women from her culture who had accomplished a great deal in their lives. Now there's a feeling that she can make changes in her life, that she can be looked upon as someone worthy of giving and receiving support.

When your girl needs exposure, don't get too worried about *where* the exposure to a new and inviting world takes place. Just make sure it does take place—and, if you can, take full advantage of the massive number of resources the Internet now makes available.

Browsing the World Wide Web together is a great (and easy) way to help your girl explore new environments. You'll find sites for specific institutions and organizations and in-depth material about subjects of interest to your girl. Try one of the popular search engines like Infoseek (www.infoseek.com) or Yahoo! (www.yahoo.com) as the first stop you and your girl can take on a trip through cyberspace.

If you're unfamiliar with the technology, or don't even have a computer, make a commitment to learn what all the fuss is about! Take a trip with your girl to a large branch of your local public library, ask a reference librarian for some basic help in getting started, and then sit down together to gather all the "cool" information you can on women's sports, architecture, songwriting, or anything else of interest to your girl. If you can't find a terminal at a mid-sized or larger library (a fairly unlikely occurrence these days), there's almost certainly someone in your own personal network who has a personal computer you can use to do some Web surfing. Jump in and learn together!

Don't pretend you have all the answers for your girl—do the exploring by her side! If you find the act of using a computer intimidating, let your own insecurity be an opportunity for deepening the girl's relationship with you. Be honest with her. Admit that you're a little overwhelmed by the prospect of wading into the Internet—and then show how you respond when you have to make sense of a new situation! Don't be surprised if your girl knows a little more about pointing and clicking than you do, and be prepared to do your learning together. In computers (and in everything else) admit what you don't know and show your girl that you're ready to acknowledge that you're not brilliant in a particular area. Then show her how you take on the challenge of exploring something new. It's okay not to know. It's not okay to make a habit of avoiding new experiences and new challenges. I always encourage mentors without lots of computer experience to take whatever steps they have to to learn how to take advantage of resources on the Internet. There are two reasons. One is that you'll find access to plenty of materials that will make the job of mentoring easier. Another is that you'll provide your girl instant access to a variety of information:

- News

- Reference works

- Great works of art

- Career advice

- Help with financial aid issues

- Statistics

- Support groups

- Internships

- Information on foreign lands

.... and (at least) ten thousand other topics of potential interest to both of you. See chapter ten for a listing of web sites that can serve as starting points for you and your girl. Use those sites to find out what's happening in the world beyond.

The wealth of information available through the Internet is truly extraordinary. It allows you and your girl to make mind-opening "journeys" without ever leaving the computer. These travels will expose your girl not only to foreign lands, but to a tidal wave of new ideas and new possibilities. This will motivate her to find out more, and getting her motivated to find out more is precisely what you're out to do. If effective learning is rooted in self-motivated exploration of topics that engage the learner, then the Internet may well be the most powerful learning environment ever developed. Don't short-change your girl—show her how to take advantage of that environment.

Another great way to open your girl's intellectual horizons is to expose her to a magazine that interests and challenges her.

I strongly suggest that you consider ordering a subscription to *blue jean magazine* ® for yourself and the girls (ages 11-21) in your life. Mercifully, *blue jean* is advertising free; it is written by teen girls for teen girls, and it celebrates intellectual development in a unique and exciting away. For subscription information, call (888) 4-blu-jean. Get your hands on a copy today—and then share it and talk about it with the girl in your life.

For young girls (ages 9-13), the best magazine may be *American Girl* ®, which presents profiles of girls from all over the country who think for themselves, take risks, and participate in fascinating activities. The magazine also offers a superior perspective on female history. For subscription information, call (800) 234-1278.

Exposure

By exposing girls to engaging, unfamiliar new worlds, we help them find their own place in the new world they create for themselves.

We can bridge the gap between the world our girls experience right now and the challenging "real world" that they're eventually going to have to enter by providing exposure to new worlds that excite them. The more girls learn about how much has been accomplished in any field they select, and how much still remains to be accomplished by people just like them, the more likely they are to get excited by the new worlds you show them. The more they learn about global environmental changes, career issues, technological changes, diversity, or whatever else interests them, the more willing they're going to be to listen to new ideas, to become challenged by them, and to act on that challenge.

Suppose there is no spark? Suppose your girl is—or appears to be—jaded, bored, and distinctly underwhelmed by just about everything in her environment? That's where you come in. You're the person in this girl's life who gets to reach out and say "Hey, wake up. This is going to be *fun*!

Follow me." Nine out of ten times, in my experience, your girl will follow you.

If I'm with a group of girls who seem to be more interested in what's happening on *Melrose Place* or *Beverly Hills 90210* than in what's happening in the world that surrounds them, I intervene. I sit them all down and start reading from *The Diary of Anne Frank*. After a while, I pass the book to one of the girls, and we take turns reading that marvelous book—a book that has never failed to resonate with any girl I've shared it with, and that vividly illustrates the existence of other worlds, other ways of living, other experiences far beyond the shallow, unrealistic depictions of mass commercial television. That book takes circumstances that are utterly different from the ones a girl is used to encountering and puts them in an emotional context she understands on a visceral level almost immediately. That's your goal as a mentor working to help expand your girl's intellectual development—to show her where those new worlds exist, and hook them into something that already has meaning for your girl.

Mentors need to be able to break existing patterns—just as the Anne Frank intervention does (and just as my Aunt Lu's decision to work with my mom to show me how to network at a party did). That's intervention. Mentors need to be able to reach out on a Saturday morning and say, "Let's go out to the historical museum today." And, by the way, that's a great setting for introducing intellectual challenge into an existing relationship!

You and your girl make the trip together—you learn what it was like to live in a certain time and place, and afterwards, perhaps while you sit together at a restaurant sharing a cup of tea, you have a discussion about the exhibit. You ask her what she thinks the biggest challenge of living in the colonial era would have been, for instance. You ask her what she would have liked best about living in that time and place. You volunteer your own thoughts about the problems women would have faced in colonial times. You might bring up high infant mortality and death-during-childbirth rates. Or perhaps you go to an art museum rather than a historical museum. What did your girl feel about the paintings she saw? Which did she like best? Why did she like it?

Challenge your girls to develop opinions, even if both of you are new to the field being discussed. You may not be an expert, but you can talk about how you feel about something you just saw. You can explore your own questions about an exhibit. You can share the experience of looking at a painting and describing it to someone else. That's what your girl needs—someone who will serve as a model when it comes time to form opinions and reactions in the face of new stimuli. Remember, you're not out to argue right and wrong—you're out to show your girl what it's like to form an opinion and discuss it.

Discussions like this help girls not only to explore the new world you've just introduced them to, but also to discover their own feelings about the time and place in which they live—its challenges, its advantages, its gender-based problems. Be prepared to follow the discussion in whatever direction it leads and be prepared to listen attentively to the questions and issues your girl raises.

"Getting out there" to take a trip to a new location (such as a museum, theater, or art exhibit) is a liberating experience in and of itself. It frees girls of habit and preconception, makes it clear that there is a huge world beyond the physical restraints of home and school, and introduces new experiences and insights. Going on trips—and talking about what we've seen—lets our daughters know that there are enviroments where it's safe, and even encouraged, to have opinions.

"The Serious Stuff"

I got a phone call recently from my sister-in-law Patti. She lives on the west coast. There are a couple of young girls in her neighborhood, and Patti does her best to reach out to them, or, as she puts it, "play with them." They do arts and crafts together or take hikes through a cornfield that's growing nearby. My sister-in-law has a Ph.D.; and the girls in her group all come from families where no one has ever gone to college. Patti has learned that, even though their parents may not have a formal education, these girls are very smart indeed. They know how to evaluate people and situations; they know how to work their way through situations. In other words, these girls have the kind of intelligence that, if it were focused in the right direction, could yield serious academic dividends.

The average age within the group is twelve. And every single one of those girls is more or less convinced that college is not in her future. It's an option that no one has ever presented.

Patti wanted an opportunity to reach out to these girls, to make a difference. She enjoyed being with them so much, and she had such clear evidence of their intellectual potential, that she couldn't imagine them not going to college. She saw how interested they were in the world around them, and she also knew she was taking part in a critical period in these girls' lives. Patti didn't want the possibility of a college education to go unexamined. She wanted to know: "How do I raise that subject? How do I get this idea onto their radar screens? How do I take advantage of their natural inquisitiveness, their strong mental focus, their hunger for knowledge—how do I take that and get them to think of college as a possible target for those energies?"

So many times, when I've met people during seminars and presentations, that's the kind of question that comes up: "How do I get them to focus on the serious stuff?" "How do I get involved in a meaningful way with the girl or girls with whom I've initiated a relationship?" "What do I do to take that potential I can see—and help to point it in a direction that will be constructive for the person I'm trying to help?"

Here's a big hint: The fact that the information you want your girls to gain exposure to is important doesn't mean it can't be fun. Don't assume what you want to talk about has to be serious. Try to keep it light; you'll stand a better chance of keeping your girl involved. Don't try to give her lists of things to do, or make demands, or issue ultimatums, or hold forth with dark predictions of what the future is going to be like if she doesn't do as you say. Make learning fun. Make it active. Make it something new.

I had a suggestion along those lines for Patti: "Try a group trip to a local university campus—not to grill the people in the admissions office, but to take advantage of something special, something the girls would like that can be found there and only there." That's exactly what she did. She and her girls made a trip to a local art exhibit that was being sponsored by the university. She might just as easily have offered to take them to a theater production, a concert, a seminar, or a demonstration at the same university. Whatever she selected, though, it had to be an event that was of genuine interest to the girls. Patti selected an art exhibit because she knew that several of her girls were fascinated by painting and sculpture.

As it turned out, that trip to the university was a great way to bring the idea of education into the picture without pulling down flip charts or launching into lectures. Now the girls are eager to learn more about what it takes to go to college. They're asking on their own.

Patti's story is an excellent example of how a mentor can support a girl's intellectual development without increasing anxiety or making demands of her that she's not ready to fulfill. Can you see how it works? Consider the following approaches in dealing with the exact same situation:

> *"You need to start thinking about college now. I think we should talk about that, and then I think we should take a trip to see exactly what you're likely to face when you finally make your way into the world of academia." (Perceived message: "You're getting to the point where you*

have to make adult choices and decisions now, and I'm going to show you how to make the right ones. You probably should have taken this step on your own already—but since you need my help to move from one phase of your development to the next, I'm willing to step in and get you the information you need.")

"Hey, there's a great-looking art exhibit over at the Rose Art Museum at the University. It looks really cool—it's about photorealism, which is something I studied in college. The painter uses a photograph as a model, and then creates paintings that look incredibly real. Want to come check it out with me this weekend?" (Perceived message: "You're important to me, and I like doing things with you. There are a lot of interesting things out there—when I run across one that looks like it might be right for an outing, you can count on me to tell you about it, so we can take a look at it together. If you've got questions, now or later, about the new environment we'll be examining together, I'm here for that.")

When it comes to encouraging intellectual development, what you *don't* say can be as important as what you do say. The emotional support you offer is as important as—no, make that more important than—the information you convey.

So ask yourself: "How can I turn this into an adventure for her—in terms she'll understand?"

If your girl has never been to a college, then she has no frame of reference about that subject. Telling her that it's something she has to "research," or demanding that she listen to you as you read from an admissions catalog, is likely to make her want to go hang out at the mall with someone who shares some of her interests. But quietly linking the idea of "college" to something your girl already likes to do—paint, say, or visit exciting new places—is a great way to elicit interest.

Mentors help to turn abstract ideas about the outside world—ideas based on notions of describing, or relaying, or imagining—into the present-tense world your girl already inhabits. You appeal to what she already knows or already wants to find out about. That's what starts conversations. That's what initiates reactions like, "Wow! How did they do that?" and "What did they make that sculpture out of?" and "What's that building over there?" And those questions, the initial questions of wonder, are the essential precursors to more specific questions about the new world you've brought into your girl's life.

"What's a campus really like?" "What do people do there?" "What kinds of classes do they teach at a big university?" "How old are people who go to college? Are they only people in their teens or twenties, or are they older, too?" "How do people pay for college?" (That's an important question, of course, and it may be phrased in any number of ways—like, for instance, "How could I do this?") The point is to get the girl to raise these questions—to initiate a dialogue, not to launch into a lengthy discourse about the pros and cons of higher education.

Launch an adventure, one that inspires a discussion. And understand, too, that while your one-on-one time with your girl is important, you shouldn't be the only one launching or supporting these adventures—mothers and fathers can play a big role in planning and encouraging the trips.

Talk It Out

Intellectual challenge doesn't just mean wandering through buildings and gazing at photographs and printed text. It means sitting down and discussing things with your girl. Intellectual challenge means talking about different cultures, bygone eras, unfamiliar industries.

One great way to follow up on a trip the two of you take is to begin a photo album together. Pick a topic that means a great deal to both of you—say, a career in medicine. Then keep an eye out for images you can save within that album that relate to the topic you've chosen. It could be a photograph of a local hospital printed from a web site, or a glossy photograph from a *Scientific American* article about a new medical procedure, or a series of drawings from a women's magazine about conducting regular breast self-examinations.

Whatever the picture is, and wherever you find it, use it to stimulate your girl's interest in the topic she's chosen to explore with you. Find a medium in which to preserve that image and capture the emotion and magic that accompanied your first discussion of it with your girl. Make the photo album project a shared project—not something you impose on your girl, but a mutually exciting, mutually engaging process of identifying and preserving images that reinforce a subject worthy of your girl's best efforts and ongoing interest.

Suppose that neither you nor your girl can travel to Nepal because of limitations on your finances. (It will probably come as no surprise that you've got a lot of company in that category!) You can still travel vicariously: look at the pictures, learn about the culture and history of Nepal, and find out as much as you can about current events in that country. Then you can talk about what you've found out—explore what your girl finds exciting, what she wants to learn next, what might lie ahead for her as she charts the next step with you. It's very important for girls to learn the skills of visualization and imagination because these skills in turn strengthen the habit of exploration. Wondering what might happen next, and finding out how to visualize it, is a critical part of intellectual development.

Your aim is to help your girl develop the kind of mind that *evaluates* information, which is not the same as simply accepting or dismissing it. Support her when she doesn't understand something. For example, help her make sense of homework that's throwing her for a loop or find someone else who can. Encourage her to ask "Why?" when she's confronted with an unfamiliar situation. This instinct to explore, to question, to establish a deep understanding, is essential to healthy development. It will also help her to clarify her own values and to develop the strength and insight she'll need to be able to access when it's time to say "No" to peer pressure that's focused on unhealthy objectives.

One of the best ways to encourage an "evaluating mind" is to ask your own "Why" questions of her at key points. These are questions that tap into her emerging moral sense and stimulate her curiosity about events and opinions—including her own.

- "Why do you think that?"

- "Why did the teacher say that?"

- "Why do you see so many women portrayed that way on TV?"

- "Why do you want to do that?"

- "Why do you think the chapter starts out that way?"

- "Why did she call her statue that?"

- "Why should we care about what happened a hundred years ago?"

- "Why do you think such-and-such is the right thing to do?'"

Raising the Stakes

The point is to help your girl learn how to explore new environments. Take an afternoon to explore some part of town both you and your girl have never visited before. Travel to a different neighborhood with an ethnic focus that's unfamiliar to your girl. Find out what your girl's experience base is, and then make a trip to a site that expands it. Such trips might include:

- A visit behind the scenes at an ethnic restaurant whose heritage is unfamiliar to your girl. (Call the owner or manager ahead of time and ask for a tour.)

- A lecture or seminar or career development work-shop that touches on an area of interest to both you and your girl. (Why make her wait until her thirties or forties?)

- A tour of a factory that makes something your girl uses or wants to learn more about. (Pharmaceutical medicines? Makeup? Construction material? It's all out there—and you can almost certainly find a facility that will show how the stuff is put together by doing some surfing with your girl on the World Wide Web.)

- A meeting with a representative of a community outreach program that is likely to inspire your girl. (One of the very best is Project Wise, a superb program offered by SUNY/Stony Brook. It encourages women scientists to act as mentors to female college students, who in turn reach out to girls in junior high and high school and encourage their participation in math and science courses. Check with your local college or university's information office to learn whether your girl may be able to take advantage of a similar program in your area.)

- A women's conference sponsored by your girl's local church. (This and similar events will help your girl to see successful women interact with each other as peers.)

- A trip to a house of worship that neither you nor your girl know much about. (Not long ago, a girl

I'm mentoring accompanied me on a trip to a Ukrainian Orthodox church, where a priest answered all our questions about the traditions of that faith and the culture of its practitioners. That trip was a real eye-opener! I'd never even been inside an Orthodox church before. Exploring a new intellectual environment with your girl can often help you explore new intellectual horizons of your own.)

- A journey to a neighborhood where the culture and ethnic heritage is markedly different from her own. (What parts of your city have you or your girl never explored? What cultural, religious, and ethnic traditions can the two of you find out more about, simply by visiting another neighborhood and wandering in and out of shops?)

You may choose to make your first journey with your girl a "safe" trip, one that exposes her to a monument or building or institution she's heard of, but never experienced firsthand. Before too long, though, you should find a way to include places that your girl has never heard of on your itinerary, places that expose her to radically different ways of living. Ideas like those outlined above represent great ways to "raise the stakes" in your efforts to establish new intellectual challenges through exposure to new worlds.

Remember, you're out to augment her experiences in the classroom, not to replace them or (even worse) to continue them as the heart of your relationship with her. Your aim is to get your girl to embrace the process of continuous learning by encouraging exposure to new environments. By, for instance, exploring religious territory that is utterly unfamiliar to her or by supporting your girl as she asks questions about Buddhism or Islam (if she's been raised in a Christian or Jewish tradition), you'll be doing much more than simply helping to fill in gaps in her knowledge base on the particular points being raised. You'll be opening your girl up to new experiences, helping her to fall in love with the very idea of learning, and encouraging her to master the skill of keeping an open mind.

Make no mistake—keeping an open mind is a skill, and it does require practice. You're the one who's going to help your girl understand that there are many different ways of, for example, reaching out to God or supporting a community that does so. While maintaining full respect for her own family's religious convictions (or absence of same), you're the one who's going to guide her through the realization that the seemingly simple, authoritative answers we are often exposed to in this life of ours may reflect realities that are a good deal more complex than they first appear.

Focusing on the Future

A while back, I read about two teenage girls who'd been arrested for murder. One was significantly older than the other; the younger girl was following the older girl's instruction. If she did as she was taught and carried out the homicide, she'd win entry into the older girl's gang.

In other words, the gang took this girl in. They made her feel wanted. They gave her a sense of belonging. They told her they would stand by her as she "learned the ropes." They promised to teach her what she had to learn to get by, but there was a catch. She had to accept the gang's values.

She did. Now she's going to jail.

She wanted to learn. She wanted a future. She was so eager to find some set of values that would sustain her in the long term that she was willing to kill for it.

How different that story could have been with just a slight change of emphasis in her life! How different it could have been if there'd been a mentor who'd been willing to step in and introduce her to a new, more constructive set of values!

If your girl is, or seems to be a possible candidate for, involvement in high-risk activities, you need to reach out immediately and help her explore the positive things the future holds for her. You need to find a way to get her excited about the possibility of exploring a career that doesn't involve hurting people, selling drugs, exploiting others, or allowing herself to be exploited. Here are some strategies that will help you do just that for girls who are in crisis or who just need a greater sense of long-term direction in their lives.

- Write her a short note. (If there's a better way to win a girl at least a temporary reprieve from her own bad habits—dangerous cliques, TV addiction, substance abuse, whatever—I don't know what it is. Take the time to write a short "just thinking about you" note that proposes face-to-face time together. Use four or five lines to let the girl know that you care about what she's going through and are eager to listen if she wants to talk about where her life is going. My Aunt Lu wrote me letters like this throughout my adolescence; they had a profound positive effect on me. For my own part as a mentor, and as someone who's written and sent a lot of these notes, I can say that I have yet to encounter a girl who didn't respond positively to one. Keep the notes brief and supportive—and keep them coming.)

- Adopt the girl as your protégé. (Take her with you to conferences, trade shows, and seminars. Introduce her to people as your protégé. Show her—first hand—how to network by walking up to complete strangers and introducing yourself to them.)

- Find something that excites and energizes your girl and then get her to commit to a career goal that relates to that field. (Again, the World Wide Web can be an invaluable resource here.)

- Sit down and work out a hypothetical career plan that makes sense for this girl. (Start by reviewing your own beginnings in the world of work. Don't come across as a know-it-all; make it clear that mistakes are part of the learning process, both in and out of the world of work. Talk about the biggest blunders you made while getting started in your career or avocation.)

- Support the development of the workplace values she'll need. (I'm talking about things like punctuality, accountability, dressing appropriately, and displaying follow-through. Your first and best approach here is to lead by example. Once the relationship is established, you may want to address extreme problem areas by such attention-getting maneuvers as: deliberately showing up late for a get-together, or skipping it altogether, and then afterwards talking about the frustration your girl felt as a result of that. Or consider scheduling—no kidding—get-togethers for 8:00 on Saturday mornings!★

- Talk about the times you completely humiliated yourself. (Sharing painful stories about the times you fell short on the job, how much it cost your career, and what you learned from your mistake, will almost always win deep interest from the girl you're mentoring.)

★ One of my earliest, and most effective, learning experiences concerning the power of appearance came when my Aunt Lu didn't make me change my supremely casual jeans-and-torn-shirt attire before we went to a formal party. She made one suggestion that I change into something more appropriate, listened to my impassioned defense of my wardrobe, and then stopped talking and took me to the party. She could have refused to take me; she could have insisted that I change clothes. She did neither. She did the smart thing, and let me experience, first-hand, how alienating it is to be dressed in the wrong clothes for a social or business gathering. It's a lesson I've never forgotten—and one that no amount of lecturing would have brought home for me.

- Support her when she fails. (This is great advice for any girl you're mentoring, of course. Don't give up on her if she doesn't follow through. Don't put the relationship in jeopardy by implying that your approval of her is dependent on her doing precisely what you say at all times. Just tell her what the problem is and move on. The message should be a simple one: "Hey, you messed up on Thursday when you didn't show up for our trip to the library [or whatever you had planned]. I'm still here for you, but I want you to know that's the kind of stuff that makes bosses angry." Don't get too fixated on outcomes, but do make sure your girl understands that she's crossed a line, and that continuing to do so in the "real world" will cost her.)

- Show her your own Day Timer or whatever other personal organizing system you use. (Show her how you keep track of the ten thousand details that are your life. Buy her one of her own and help her start to use it—and let her know there's no sin in rescheduling something!)

- When in doubt, simply ask—"What do you want to be doing five years from now? Okay—what can we do together to help make that happen?" (As you work to help your girl focus on career issues, remember that you're playing for the long term. Again, give your girl the opportunity to mess things up a few times; make it clear that you're willing to stand by her, even when she falls down. Show her—by your example—that the real genius isn't the person who never makes a mistake, but the person who knows how to try again after the mistake.)

Making Learning a Life-Long Endeavor

Too many of our daughters emerge from our educational system believing that learning stops once someone earns a diploma of some kind. Your job is to convince your girl that learning is an experience that strong women embrace throughout their lives. The best way to do this, as I've pointed out again and again in this chapter, is to take your girl by the hand and experience an unfamiliar world with her, serving as a model for the learning process itself—and appealing to the natural curiosity and inquisitiveness of youth.

Whether that means helping your girl get a head start on writing a resume, letting her watch a capable, experienced woman who knows how to run a restaurant, or convincing her to attend a line-dancing class for the first time, you need to help her become comfortable with the idea of exposing herself to something new. Once she falls in love with the act of learning about a brand new way of thinking, she'll realize that she's got access to all kinds of resources, as many as she can imagine. Once girls realize how vast and exciting the world really is, they don't have to be talked into learning. They get hooked on learning. And once they're hooked on learning, they start to learn how valuable they themselves really are.

6

The Third Essential : Emotional Development

No discussion of mastering the art of growing up would be complete without a look at the difficult question of how mentors can support girls and young women in their own emotional growth.

For most women, emotional mastery is a lifelong process, not a job that's completed and crossed off a list for good during adolescence. Still, well-adjusted women do learn how to manage their emotions, rather than letting their emotions manage them.

Grown women who develop day-to-day coping and survival skills may sometimes forget how devastating the process of coming of age emotionally can feel, and they may not realize how awesome the implications of emotionally-driven choices may eventually turn out to be for today's young women. Serving as the mentor to a girl or young woman will serve as an effective refresher course on the many challenges of emotional development as adulthood approaches.

In a world where peer pressure is often intense, and where experimentation with sex, alcohol, drugs, and crime is commonplace, the stakes are very high indeed for our daughters. They need to be able to make the best possible choices when the time comes, and they need to learn that first instincts, despite their strength, are not necessarily the best instincts. In short, our daughters need effective role models as they learn how to navigate the (initially frightening) emotional landscapes of adulthood. Without regular interaction with a well-adjusted nonparental female adult— a mentor who encourages and supports healthy emotional growth—the vast majority of girls and young women will, I believe, find themselves exposed to developmental and social risks they simply shouldn't have to face. Before they've learned to make sense of their own suddenly unpredictable emotional reactions, before they've come to terms with the startling force of some of the new feelings that are emerging in their lives, they'll be pressured into making decisions for which they're unprepared. The paths they choose may well be ones that they—and the people who love them—end up regretting for years to come.

Riding the Emotional Wave

What are emotions? Most of us know what they are on an intuitive level, but defining emotions in black-and-white terms can be a tricky business. I think it's worth trying to establish a working definition of the word "emotions" before we proceed further.

As far as I can see, emotions are the array of perceptions, feelings, thoughts, and beliefs about ourselves that either empower us or paralyze us. They're the waves we ride, day in and day out. They're what a great poet called "the raw materials whence we mold our lives."

Despite what we may like to tell ourselves from time to time, human beings are inherently emotional creatures. When we are overrun by feelings of despair, anger, resentment, frustration, or stress, we are likely to make poor choices. When we're energized, buoyant, optimistic, and calm, we tend to do better with the challenges we face. It's a common observation that most decisions to purchase something are made on an emotional level—and justified on a rational level. This is why television advertisements, for instance, usually rely far more heavily on emotional appeals to our feelings of, say, status, belonging, embarrassment, pride, or sexual attraction than they do to a "nothing but the facts" assessment of product advantages and disadvantages. I'll go further and say that the vast majority of all human decisions have strong emotional motivations, and that we offer logical rationalizations of our "gut feelings" so often, and so unconsciously, that the very idea of "acting rationally" is usually an exercise in benign self-delusion. We may assess our decisions rationally, but I think that, in day-to-day life, the vast majority of people use their powers of logical analysis to confirm the validity of "instinctive" positions they're already predisposed to take.

Think back, then, for just a moment—and recall how intimidating and tumultuous life was when *your* emotions were likely to shift from day to day, hour to hour, or even moment to moment! No wonder we often felt, as young girls, as though the ground beneath us was rumbling and splitting under our feet. Our decision-making mechanisms—our structures for developing choices about how we would interact with the world around us—were under construction, but we still had to use them!

Women are led to believe that they're the "more emotional" of the two genders. I think that's something of an oversimplification. My feeling is that we're less skilled at covering up emotional reactions than men, and that we're more inclined than men to seek emotional support from other people—and to provide that support in turn. We tend to have greater empathy for others than men do and to place a higher level of importance on the challenge of relating to other people and understanding them. We appear also to spend more of our time depressed than men do, a fact that may simply be a consequence of the importance we attach to our relationships with other people (both male and female), relationships that have both their up days and their down days.

I don't accept the idea that emotions necessarily play an overriding or primary role in the life of the average woman, but I do accept the notion that emotional connections and reactions represent an important part of who we are. (Put another way, I don't think any living human being, male or female, is one-dimensional enough to be described accurately as "primarily emotional.")

Managing Our Emotions: A Basic Coping Skill

Most of us are quite capable of having a stupendously bad day, the kind of day that leaves us feeling emotionally overwhelmed. By the same token, though, most of us know that these days don't last forever, and we somehow find ways to rebound from them.

Since just about all of us have learned, at some level, how to "keep on keeping on," (as it were) I think it's fair to say that just about any of us can serve as models for effective emotional self-management. As in so many other areas where mentors can make a difference, you shouldn't try to be perfect. You should just try to be you.

My own feeling is that just about every woman manages to develop effective coping and self-management mechanisms. These are the tools that help her step back and get some perspective during times of high stress, sudden reversal, and, yes, when experiencing hormonal changes associated with monthly menstrual cycles. In my view, the question is not whether your girl will develop a set of emotional self-management skills, but *when* she will develop those skills.

So why is a mentor necessary at all? Because, among girls, and especially among teenagers, effective self-maintenance on an emotional level happens much more quickly and more effectively when a mentor is there to show how it's done. That's my experience based on years of work with hundreds of girls. They catch on more quickly when an adult woman other than their mothers shows them how to manage their emotional states.

This leads to a natural conclusion: If your girl develops emotional coping tools more quickly with you than she would without you, she's better off learning from you sooner rather than later. With your guidance and support, she's less likely to engage in risky and/or self-destructive behaviors. In other words, you want your girl to learn how to step back from the situation and take a deep breath when she's fifteen and hasn't, for instance, had sex yet, rather than when she's seventeen and has two children to take care of. If the learning process we're talking about takes place when she's seventeen, then your girl begins to learn how to get through the day, despite all the extraordinary pressures associated with being a young single mother. If the learning process takes place when she's fifteen, your girl stands a better chance of avoiding becoming a young single mother in the first place.

Emotional Crises

I'm often asked about the single best way to initiate a mentor relationship with a girl who appears to be experiencing serious emotional problems. There are two steps to keep in mind here: first, consult a qualified professional therapist or social worker. Explain the situation to this person and ask for advice. (In other words, don't get in over your head by offering therapeutic advice you're not qualified to give.) Second, by all means *reach out* in a way that allows the girl to understand, immediately and with no demands of reciprocity, that someone cares about her. Follow the advice I mentioned in the previous chapter: Write a brief note and pop it into the mail. Don't pass judgment or take a condescending tone about anything. Use just a couple of lines to let the girl you're concerned about know that you care about what's happening in her life, that you'd like to share some time with her, that you're a great listener, and that you're convinced that the two of you would have a great time together.

Such an approach may sound simple—too simple—but that kind of letter can be, quite literally, a lifesaver. Write it, send it, and follow up on it with a phone call *before* your girl's situation takes a turn for the worse.

Show Your Girl How to Reach Out

Show your girl, by example, that it's possible for women to put the events in their lives in perspective most of the time—and that there's nothing wrong with reaching out to other people on those rare occasions when you feel as though you *can't possibly* put things in perspective.

Your girl may have unrealistic assumptions or expectations about her own emotional reactions. She may consider an entirely normal transition period to show signs of profound instability or inexcusable vulnerability on her part. By the same token, she may mistake a sudden, momentary rush of feeling—anger or joy or heartbreak—for the last word on the realities she faces in her life. It's also quite possible that she will, at least in early adolescence, feel that there's something inherently wrong about admitting that she needs to reach out to someone other than her mother or father— despite the fact that every fiber of her being may be urging her to reach out to someone other than her mother or father. On an emotional level, your job is to show her how to either a) handle the many pressures she faces on her own, or b) reach out to someone else (say, you) when she's feeling confused or overwhelmed. That's your job.

In all likelihood, you'll find it's easiest in the early going to encourage your girl to reach out to you during tough times. Once you've developed a certain comfort level with one another, perhaps shortly after your first or second walk/jog/bike ride/whatever, there will come a point when your girl will come to you with a crisis. Encourage her to talk; encourage her to cry or scream or whisper; encourage her to reach out to you. She's learning how to connect with another woman about events in her life that make a difference.

That's a valuable skill, one that you should definitely pass along. But you must be careful. The skill you're teaching is that of reaching out and building emotional alliances with other women—not transferring emotional needs from one parental figure to another. Trying to replace your girl's mother as a source of emotional support is a huge mistake. The best way to avoid doing this is to find some way to highlight your own vulnerability and need for emotional support from key people in your life (other than your girl!).

Not long ago, I sat down with some of the girls who are in my Girl Scout troop. We were having an afternoon snack; they arrived as scheduled at my office and had seen me getting very frustrated about a problem I was facing about an upcoming seminar. I made a conscious decision to let them see me have the bad day that was already well underway. Why not? I was already deeply rattled, and I had been promising myself for some time that I'd find some way to make it clear to them that I was a human being, a person who needed support from time to time.

I may have been telling only half the truth when I said that the day had left me "frustrated." What the girls had seen was me getting so bent out of shape over a business relationship that didn't develop in quite the way that I wanted it to, that I broke down and cried after hanging up the telephone. They'd seen me at the end of a perfectly abysmal day; I was stressed out and definitely not at my best. They'd seen me with my tank empty and my flat tire galumphing pathetically as I cruised over to the breakdown lane. They'd seen me lose it.

I don't lose it often—but I am human, and I do lose it from time to time. A lot of people I know have the good sense to keep crying once they've started crying. This time, I decided to follow their example. (I remember seeing a *Peanuts* cartoon some years back in which a wailing Lucy, told not to cry by a sympathetic Charlie Brown, responds with something along the lines of, "What? And deprive myself of a perfectly healthy emotional outlet?") By choosing to continue my crying jag, despite the fact that the girls were in the room, I was also deciding to put into practice my belief that mentors should not try to exemplify perfection in their every encounter with the girls they help. So when my husband David walked into the room, I did what I would normally do in that situation. I asked him for a hug.

It's sometimes embarrassing or frustrating to have to ask for help. But it's part of being a grownup. I think it was very important for the girls to see me ask David for a hug after that difficult call. I think it was very important that they realize that real, live women have real emotions. I think it was very important that they understand that women like me—women like you—sometimes bump up against things that seem overwhelming and don't make sense, that grown-up women sometimes react strongly to those things, that they know how to ask for support, and that they receive that support. Of course, it was also important that they see me reassemble myself after that difficult call. And it was important that they learn that real, live women out in the big bad world can work miracles. Not the miracle of never getting the wind knocked out of them, but the even greater miracle of knowing how to "keep on keeping on" when they find themselves gasping for air.

After I'd settled down, Louise, one of the girls, started talking about her own mom, about how stressed out she gets sometimes, how she breaks down in tears, and how that left her feeling confused and lost when it happened. So we talked about that, how people get wound up in their work or their home life from time to time, how things can seem larger than they are when you're trying to accomplish a great deal. I talked about what I'd felt during my phone call, and what I imagined Louise's mom felt at the end of a long day. I also talked about how it was a pretty good bet that both of us needed hugs from time to time. I talked about what it's like to try to hold a family together, as a working mom or as a stay-at-home mom. (I explained to her that I have some experience on this front, as I've played both roles during the course of my life.)

Perhaps most important, I talked to Louise about how moms want to be so perfect, how we want to do everything just right and keep everyone happy. I explained how that desire to do everything as perfectly as we possibly can has its good side—it helps countless families stay strong, certainly—but I also explained how it can also cause the mom who's experiencing that desire to stretch herself too thin from time to time.

I didn't explain any of this as a "Seasoned Expert on What Constitutes Right and Wrong Behavior in the Home," or as someone Louise had viewed through the prism of her own family. I talked about my own experience as a woman, about my own vulnerabilities and excesses, about my own feeling of stress, about my own desire to keep everyone happy. This led to a really remarkable discussion about the girls' feelings on these same issues: In the aftermath of my crying jag and Louise's admission of confusion and alienation when confronted with her mother's crying, all the girls started to open up about what it means to be a mother, what it means to be a daughter, and what it means to need help and not want to ask for it. They spoke up about their hopes of making a better life for themselves, their occasional inclinations toward perfectionism, their feelings of a lack of balance, their intense desire to accomplish things, and their equally intense frustrations when things didn't turn out exactly as they'd planned.

Different Girls, Different Needs

I learned a lot from that conversation. I learned that there are some girls like Louise who find occasional expressions of emotion scary, perhaps because the whole topic of emotional expression on an adult level is now pretty intimidating. I learned that there are girls like Karen, who are so familiar with their mother's carefully maintained persona of perfectionism that they come to think of her as someone who *never* needs to ask for help—or, at the very least, someone who offers support and love first and asks for help second. In many families, that's the definition of a mother: Someone who comforts and doesn't require comforting in turn. (That may be a limiting and perhaps even suffocating definition, but it is, in my experience, common just the same.) And I learned that there are girls like Joan who, because of the intense emotional stakes involved when a mother expresses an emotional need of some kind, feel alienated and distressed when they see evidence of their own mother emerging from a bad day.

None of these girls had the "right" approach—none of them was "wrong." All three were encountering real life, and real emotions, and realizing how much power and energy emotions carry with them.

Mentor relationships should include first-hand examples of how grownups handle difficult and trying turns of fate. As a mentor, you should be ready to demonstrate, not that you never feel intimidated, but that you know how to deal with the feeling of intimidation. You should be ready to model how healthy women respond to setbacks and stress, how they process those all too common phenomena of modern life, and how they get back on the saddle again once the worst has passed.

Girls need to realize that part of being a mature woman is encountering pain and hardship and disappointment, dealing with it, and then moving on. If they don't see this process first-hand, they may make the assumption that some women manage to live lives that *never* have moments of stress, anger, disappointment, or misunderstanding. And they may measure themselves against that impossible standard, find themselves wanting, and suffer as a result. Show them the real stuff. Show them the tough moments of your life—and show your strategies for finding support and coping, too. Once you've made it clear to your girl that your relationship to her is very different from that of a mother, you'll probably want to ask her for a hug now and then. This will accomplish two important goals:

1. *It will reinforce the message that you're a human being who needs emotional support every now and then; and*

2. *It will demonstrate, in a dramatic and unmistakable way, that it is okay for the girl to ask you for a hug when things get rough—which they will.*

To be allowed to break down and cry when you're incredibly tense, to be able to ask for support, to be able to get it—these are important human victories. They're victories girls should be able to experience first-hand—without having to unravel, at the same time, momentous emotional questions along the lines of The True Nature of My Mother. Let's be honest: Accepting one's parents' humanity and fallibility—whether they were as incredibly supportive as my mother, or as silent and absent as my father, is one of life's more difficult lessons. It's not surprising, then, that girls need role models other than their parents when it comes to developing their own emotional maintenance skills.

Girls should be able to accept that bad days happen to them and to others. Mentors can share the realities of their day to day lives and talk about setbacks and frustrations in a way that's not scary. Mentors can say, "Hey, this is what you're going to have to deal with. This is how I deal with it. You need to learn how to deal with it in a way that makes sense for you." For a variety of reasons, that message is sometimes easier to hear coming from someone who doesn't play the role of parent in your girl's life.

How Do I Respond?

It's very important for girls and young women to get pragmatic messages about coping skills from mentors. Those messages serve as a stepping-stone to the development of their own basic emotional coping skills. I can attest that many, many girls find themselves in highly stressful situations—and have no experience base whatsoever for dealing with the powerful emotions that accompany those situations.

The kind of girl I'm talking about simply has no meaningful role model, parental or otherwise, when it comes to handling emotional pressures. This girl has never seen anybody cope with emotional overload. She's never had anybody ask anybody else for a hug. (For many girls, it's a rarity for an adult to *offer* a completely supportive hug.) She's never seen anybody ask for support and then set about the task of reassembling herself so she can reassemble her world. As a result, she may lack certain essential "self-reassembly" skills.

I realize that the picture I'm painting may seem melodramatic, but rest assured that, for many girls, it's absolutely accurate. Girls and young women need mentors for lots of reasons, but one of the most important is that they often lack any effective role model who will show them how to deal with powerful (and inevitable) emotions constructively. If girls lack that role model, there's a very good chance that they'll find themselves struggling.

Even when you feel as though you can't possibly share meaningful lessons with the girl or young woman in your life, you can share one of the most valuable lessons of them all: What to do when you're absolutely sure you've reached the end of your rope. It's imperative that you show that emotional peaks and valleys are part of life itself—and that they don't represent a personal failing of some kind or a personal catastrophe.

People have problems. People find ways to get over them. Perhaps you saw the episode of *Mad About You* in which Helen Hunt's character, at the end of a very bad day, shares a couple of less-than-optimistic insights with a young wife-to-be who happens to be sitting next to her in a hairdresser's waiting room. Hunt's character starts ranting against the institution of marriage as a whole—and weighs in with

some memorable zingers about housework, sexual dissatis-
faction, and the physical changes associated with childbirth.
In other words, she focuses on the negative and thoroughly
traumatizes the young woman, who decides to call off her
upcoming wedding! Later in the program, after some
prompting, Hunt makes a point of telling her young charge
that, despite her earlier bad mood, her decision to get married
and have children was the best choice of her entire life. (The
skittish bride-to-be eventually opts for the aisle once again.)

This was a rare—and effective—instance of television
offering a glimpse of a fundamental emotional reality. Adult
relationships aren't always easy. Motherhood isn't always
easy. Sometimes we have horrible days; sometimes we need
to vent. After we vent for a bit, we pick up our lives from
where we left off. I would argue that both halves of a life are
important for girls and young women to see. Either half in
isolation—the constant, unresolved tension or anguish, or
the carefully maintained facade of perpetual self-control
that never slips—is unhealthy.

Encourage Healthy Interchanges

Mothers and fathers, of course, have an immensely important role to play when it comes to modeling effective
emotional coping mechanisms. One of the strongest supporting factors for developing the ability to maintain a
successful relationship as an adult, for instance, is to have
seen one's parents fight—and not just fight, but also resolve
key issues by seeing the fight through. Watching one's

mother and father attack each other endlessly or bicker as a primary means of communication, of course, is *not* a good signal to send; the luckiest of our daughters get to watch their parents use solid coping and negotiation skills to make sense of the inevitable conflicts that arise from time to time in any healthy relationship. But not all of our girls are lucky enough to have that model in their homes as they grow up.

I'd argue that the same advantage exists for girls and young women who see their own mentors display personal coping skills during the difficult stretches that are part of any human life. If our daughters see these skills in action, they'll realize that everyone needs a hug now and then, and they'll feel better about asking someone in their support network for one. If they see us working through a problem with a colleague, overcoming a conflict or defusing an attack, then they'll realize that healthy relationships—personal and professional—are relationships that can withstand pressure and discord.

Let your girl know that you have real, live emotional needs. Share your coping skills—or discover some new ones and tell her about what you've learned. For instance,

- Take a walk by yourself.

- Write down all of your thoughts, feelings, and emotions about a painful topic, and either burn them in a pot, or rip up the page and bury the pieces.

- Read a meditation book and meditate on what an appropriate response to the situation could be; wait patiently for an answer.

- Take an aerobics class, ride a bike, or hit a boxing pillow.

- Exchange foot massages. (My sister-in-law and I find this to be a superior anxiety/stress/ "I'm-having-a-lousy day" reliever.)

- Call someone you love to talk to.

- Play with your own pet—or go to a pet store and play with a puppy or kitten.

- Read *The Aladdin Factor* by Jack Canfield, Mark Victor Hansen, and Patty Hansen.

Emotional Turmoil

After my father left my life when I was twelve, with no warning or explanation, I frequently found myself in tears. I would ask myself all kinds of questions that didn't seem to have any rational answers at all. What awful thing had I done? Why had this happened to me? How could God allow this to happen? Didn't he see that it wasn't fair? I can remember lying in bed for so many nights with my head buried beneath the blankets, feeling so much frustration, anger, confusion, and fear. I was in the middle of a problem I couldn't understand.

Though the specifics of the problems that countless young women and girls face today are different, the situation is essentially the same. They have to make sense of things that a great many adults would have a hard time making sense of: abandonment, sexual abuse, rape, alcohol or substance abuse on the part of a parent or close family member, and any number of other challenges. Add to these the extraordinary emotional pressures that accompany a normal adolescence (if there is such a thing): visible physical changes, hormonal shifts, intense peer pressure, the onset of menstruation, and so on.

Girls face an incredible set of emotional challenges. I know, because I did when I was a girl. I wish I'd had someone to talk me through my rage at my situation, but for many years, I didn't. It was hard for me to create any kind of stability in my life. I had no idea what to do with the intense emotions that had suddenly arisen. All I knew was that suddenly I had big problems. And it wasn't fair.

As a result of conversations I had with mentors who tried to reach out to me (notably my Aunt Lu), I started, slowly, to come to terms with the fact that *life* sometimes isn't fair. And, indeed, that is one of the most important lessons of adolescence—that we cannot always appeal to someone to make life fair for us. But even though I was able to begin to make some headway toward understanding this lesson during my mid-teens, I still felt a powerful sense of rage, of having been cheated, of having been manipulated. In my more lucid moments, I realized that the people I was angriest at were my father, for having left me, and my uncle, for having tried to rape me. But recognizing the targets for that anger didn't make the anger go away.

In my later teens, I enrolled in a lot of college courses that were meant to encourage self-confidence and self-awareness. One of those classes was in acting. I didn't know it when I showed up on the first day, but that class would change my life forever.

The instructor was a sweet, attentive woman named Carol who had (oddly, I thought at the time) recruited me quite intently shortly after my freshman orientation. Looking back on it now, I think she must have sensed from our early discussions together that I could benefit from what her class had to offer.

The early sessions went for hours and hours, and featured many exercises designed to help us learn to trust each other and cohere as a group. Trust, I learned, was essential to acting—and Carol worked hard to get us to share vulnerabilities, talk openly about fears and past problems, and generally learn to support each other as members of the emerging troupe we were.

For some unfathomable reason, this acting teacher started talking to us all about forgiveness. I remember thinking to myself that she must have gone off the deep end. The trust and sharing exercises were all very well. They probably had some practical purpose in the later work we'd be doing together as actors. But why on earth would it benefit any of us to start talking about people from our own past who needed our forgiveness?

Carol knew—as I did not yet know—that some form of forgiveness is essential to the trust that makes good ensemble acting possible. I realize now that she also understood that forgiveness was an essential prerequisite to leading a life as a whole person.

She said again and again—often looking my way as she said it—that in order for us to move on to the next levels of our lives, in order to develop into people who are capable of enough compassion to work with others in the theater, we all had to learn the art of forgiving.

She gathered us all in a circle, and each of us spoke in turn about the person in our life we most needed to learn how to forgive. When there were awkward silences—and there were plenty—Carol would tell us *why* we were doing what we were doing. She reminded us that the act of forgiving takes time and attention, and that it's among the most selfish, and healthy, things you can possibly do for yourself. Carol's brand of forgiveness had no religious overtones, no choirs or abstractions. It was supremely practical. It had a goal: to help the forgiver reassume her own birthright of peace and tranquility.

Carol helped us all to understand that you didn't try to work through to forgiveness because you approved in any way of what the person who needed forgiving had done to you. You tried to work your way through to forgiveness because you yourself needed to get back to a sense of owning your own life.

Listening to Carol, I found myself understanding what the root of the word "forgiving" meant—or at least what it meant to me. It meant getting the most possible value back out of my life by *giving* something. It meant reaching a conclusion, deeply held and carefully considered, in order to give away the rage and frustration I had felt toward two men in my life who had let me down in tragic ways.

When my turn to talk came around, Carol looked me right in the eyes and encouraged me to take all the time I needed to talk about forgiveness. And I did. It wasn't easy, and it wasn't quick, but I talked and talked, and finally started to let go of the anger and rage I felt toward my father and my uncle.

The classes went on for two long days—a Saturday and a Sunday. It was a shattering weekend, and one of the most important experiences of my life. Speaking in front of (former) total strangers about events that had left me furious to the point of incapacitation had somehow helped me to come out the other side. I realized how much of what I was doing in my life was based on my fury at people who weren't around anymore, who wouldn't know how I felt no matter what happened. And yet I was expending huge amounts of energy toward hating them—and hurting myself in the process.

Forgiveness happened for me that weekend. It probably couldn't have happened a year or two beforehand. I know with all my heart that it wouldn't have happened if I hadn't had Carol there, willing to listen as I talked my way through everything that had happened to me, how I felt about it, and what I planned to do next. What Carol did for me, you may be able to do for a girl in crisis—if you're careful, supportive, and extremely attentive, just as she was for me.

Understand that talking one's way through to forgiveness is usually a long-term process, one that progresses in stages and grows out of simply being listened to. Understand that you can't pressure anyone into forgiving someone she's not ready to forgive. Understand that you may have to raise the idea and pose a few carefully selected, challenging questions (as Carol did)—but know when to back off. And finally, understand that neither you nor your girl should expect forgiveness to happen overnight.

We should expect it to happen eventually, though, and we should be willing to have the talks, smile through the occasional silences, and, when the moment is right, ask the questions that will help our daughters let go of the poison of rage before it kills them. We should be willing to ask the kinds of questions Carol asked me:

- If you could change one event in your life, what would that event have been?

- How did that event make you feel?

- What do you think about that event now?

- How does that event affect your life now?

- If you could say anything to the person who hurt you, anything at all, what would you say?

Carol, who was a genius at that kind of patient, supportive questioning, is still my role model for dealing with girls who hold on to rage. She still reminds me, after all these years, that our role as mentors in helping girls deal with turbulent emotions is to help them understand that the only thing we can affect in this life is our own perceptions of situations. We may not have control over what happened to us in the past, but we do have control over the way we deal with people now. Other people are responsible for their own actions. We can't change them—not by pretending that they are something that they're not, and not by harboring anger against them, stoking it up in our hearts at every opportunity. We can only change the way we look at the situations that face us.

If you are preparing to help a girl deal with the ramifications of trauma, violation, or betrayal, you will need to summon resources of patience and good humor—and you will need to be able to recognize when your girl is not yet ready to confront the "literal" truth of her situation. Attacking or confronting a girl, demanding that she "face the facts" about personal crises, is almost always a hallmark of ineffective mentoring. If you're not a therapist or psychologist (or even if you are), you should know that there are times when a girl needs to confront her problems in her own way, and that, given the chance, she can usually be counted on to face up to the realities of her life at her own pace, and on her own terms, when a supportive adult makes a commitment to listen to her.

Carol helped me to embrace the values that support a classic prayer first formulated by Reinhold Niebuhr. This prayer should guide any and all efforts to help your girl talk through feelings of rage and frustration resulting from problems in her past. It can serve as an invaluable support to both you and your girl.

"Lord, grant me the serenity to accept the things that I cannot change, the courage to change the things that I can change, and the wisdom to know the difference."

Between Two Worlds

One reason emotional storms can seem so difficult to your girl may be that she's in transition between two very different emotional worlds. As a mentor, you can play a vital role in helping her leave one behind and enter another, while dealing constructively with the inevitable feelings of inadequacy or vulnerability that accompany the transition.

When she was younger—six, seven, eight years old—your girl was not in a position to change people or events. She was a child, the center of her universe, and whether or not she actually received the care she deserved, she probably had a sense, as most children do, that she *should* have been cared for, just as she was. That's the ideal during childhood: Parents, friends, teachers, and loved ones are there to support us, just as we are.

Then, as adolescence dawns, the dynamic starts to change. All of a sudden, your girl finds herself preparing for the world of adulthood, the world of obligations. Change is everywhere: in schoolwork, in relationships with parents, in interactions with peers. People don't simply take care of her every need. Those in the adult world have responsibilities, and with every new, two-way relationship she undertakes, your girl takes another step into that world. Suddenly, it seems as though the world is out to change your girl and everything with which she's become familiar. She feels as though she has no control over her environment.

Adolescents in general, and girls in particular, tend to react with very strong emotional responses to this shift from an "I'll take care of you" mode of living to an "obligations and responsibilities" mode of living. She's likely to feel threatened, intimidated, and even betrayed—and she's probably going to want to change the very people and situations that seem to demand her to change.

As your girl's mentor, you are the bridge between the parental "I'll take care of you" mode and the "I'll do this for you, you do this for me" mode your girl will be establishing with peers and adults. You are the transition point, and a large part of your job is to help her understand that, even though it's natural for her to have strong feelings about situations, simply having the feelings won't change the situation, as they often did during childhood. That's one of the fundamental lessons of adulthood, and you'll be teaching it to her—by your example first, your listening skills second, and your words third—in countless ways as your relationship progresses.

There are some emotional transitions that your girl simply won't be able to share with her parents. She's going to share them with you. Let her. Don't be frightened away if what you hear is intense, contradictory, or confusing.

A note to parents who may be reading this chapter: It's quite common for some mothers to feel pangs of jealousy when they realize that their daughter is sharing feelings and problems with another person. This is a completely natural response—but remember that your daughter has a developmental need to create independence and become self-sufficient, and that part of the process by which this occurs is the creation of confidences that don't include parents. It's not a question of *whether* your girl will share emotional responses with someone other than you, but whom she'll share those responses with. By working to support your daughter's relationship with a mentor who shares your values, you'll be taking the most positive, constructive step you can to help her grow emotionally (and in the other four essential areas, as well). When mentors hear the difficult issues your daughter is dealing with, that's a positive step for everyone. It means that your daughter is not turning inward and suffering alone, but rather is asking for help.

Mentors can best provide that help by following four basic rules.

Rule One: Let Her Vent

As a mentor, you can't explain away your girl's feelings—she's going to have to experience them. When in doubt, simply listen to her. If she has to rant for a while, let her get it out of her system.

Let her know that you will always offer her a safe place to talk, a place where she won't be told that her feelings are silly or immature or invalid or unrealistic. If it's important enough for her to express, it's important enough for you to listen. And if it's important enough for her to cry, or scream, or shout, or whine for protracted periods, it's important enough for you to support. Show that you're willing to stand by her without judging her as a person, even at difficult moments.

Don't try to resolve, conclude, or prioritize. Let your girl do that. As is so often the case, the simple act of allowing your girl to express herself freely is often the best way to help her arrive at her own solutions. You may, at appropriate moments (such as a lengthy pause), choose to introduce questions that encourage her to explore her emotions a little more deeply, such as the questions focused on forgiveness that we examined a little earlier in this chapter. But for the most part, you're going to let her vent. In many cases, your girl is going to conclude her monologue with some variation on the question, "Well, what do *you* think I should do?" That's when it's time to follow...

Rule Two: When Pressed for Advice, Introduce the A-B-C-D System

Respond to your girl's question by asking something along the following lines: "Well, would you like to learn about something I use when I'm feeling stressed out?" In order to make that appeal honestly, of course, you have to be willing to practice the system that follows in your own life. You may already do so on an intuitive basis, but I urge you now to formalize that process and apply the ideas that appear below to deal with emotional challenges in your own life. It's an effective way to get perspective on such powerful emotions as anger, fear, intense physical attraction, or self-doubt. Both you and your girl stand to benefit greatly by learning how to respond to emotional challenges through what I call the A–B–C–D system.

STEP A: ACKNOWLEDGE. Recognize that you are experiencing a strong emotion. The first and greatest problem most of us face in dealing with powerful emotions is our own failure to recognize that emotional states have a strong impact on our perceptions. So step A has to do with acknowledging.

Step away from the situation. Take a deep breath. Catalogue exactly what you're feeling. How does your body react to this situation? Does your neck feel more tense when you're fearful? Does your breathing become shallow when you're stressed out? If there's a feeling of physical attraction toward someone, do you suddenly notice tingling or rushing sensations in various parts of your body? Examine these realities, catalogue the physical changes you feel when you're under the influence of the emotion in question. How our bodies react has a huge impact on our emotional responses to situations. Notice those responses—don't accept them automatically as the best (or only) barometer of the circumstances you face.

STEP B: BREATHE. Take a deep breath. Close your eyes. Count to ten slowly. Then ask yourself silently, while still keeping your eyes closed and your breath slow and steady: Exactly what role am I playing in this situation? What factors are under my control? What are my options?

STEP C: CONTEMPLATE. This is where you examine elements of the situation and assess whether they are within your control or beyond your control. Open your eyes and look around. Ask yourself: What's really going on? If there's another person involved in this situation, what is motivating his or her behavior? If there's a possibility of physical danger, how long do you have before you must take action to deal with it in one way or another?

STEP D: DECIDE. This is where you make a conscious choice to pursue the path that makes the most sense for you as a person. If necessary, review the situation more deeply. Consider all the options you developed in the previous step. Then decide: How should you proceed from here? What steps should you take to deal with this situation in a way that preserves your own integrity and leads to the best long-term outcome for you? How and when can you evaluate this decision later on? Determine whether it still makes sense for you. (Remember: Making decisions means making your own best choices using your own free will.)

The A–B–C–D system for addressing strong emotional states is a powerful, effective strategy that can help your girl make sense of potentially devastating situations in which her own strong feelings may not support the decision that's in her own best interests. In my counseling work, both formal and informal, I've dealt with hundreds of girls who've walked into my office or living room and started venting about the most extraordinary things: boyfriend problems, parent problems, thoughts of suicide, wardrobe dilemmas, you name it. The A–B–C–D system, once it's been practiced a time or two, has always helped them gain perspective and insight on the challenges they faced. It's the single best tool I can pass along to you for emotional self-management ... to use in your own life and pass along to your girl. When you teach girls how to use it, and explain how it's helped you make sense of the emotional challenges in your own life, they're much less likely to cede control of their decision-making process to the gusts of their own emotional storms.

Practice A–B–C–D yourself. Develop your own set of success stories. Then walk your girl through the process when she asks you for help in dealing with a situation that's left her feeling as though she's lost control of her life. A–B–C–D will help her isolate exactly what she does have control over. Following the A–B–C–D system will help her accept that she can't change the way friends or parents feel; help her identify and extricate herself from dangerous or abusive or manipulative situations before they become serious; and help her develop the sense of confidence that comes with improving one's decision-making skills.

Not long ago, Deborah, a fourteen-year-old girl I've been mentoring, shared a story that illustrates A–B–C–D in action. As it happened, she had taught the A–B–C–D process to two of her friends; the three girls had received permission from their parents to attend a party at a friend's house. There were boys at the party, and the parents who were supposed to be supervising the get-together stepped out and left the kids on their own. (Score one demerit for that couple!) The kids started playing party games, and one of the classics—spin-the-bottle—soon became the focus of the group's attention.

The kids spun the bottle. The kids started kissing each other, as the rules of the game demanded. Before long, a few pairs of kids—including my girl's friends—made their way to bedrooms or dens to be alone for awhile. The game continued; Deborah took her first turn, spun the bottle, and realized that the game now "demanded" that she kiss a boy who had been eyeing her with some interest—and whom she realized she found quite appealing.

That's when it happened.

As she explained the moment to me later, she realized that she was facing an emotionally-powerful situation. She started by *acknowledging* that her emotions were running high, and that there were strong physical changes in her body. Then she closed her eyes and *breathed*. She counted to ten, won a certain distance from the situation, and started thinking about the parts of the situation that were still under her control. Then she *contemplated* what would happen under various scenarios. She played out all the potential scenarios— what might happen if she extracted herself from the game and called her mother to ask for a ride home, if she leaned over and kissed the boy she was "supposed" to kiss under the "rules" of the game, or if she did nothing and let someone else take a turn. Finally, she reviewed all of her options and *decided* to take the course of action that seemed to her to lead to the best outcome. She stood up, walked to the phone, and called her mother to ask for a ride home. The story gets even better. My girl's two friends heard her making the call—and realized that their own best options were to accompany her into the car and ask for rides home. They had been conducting their own A-B-C-D sessions at the same time my girl had!

Rule Three: When You Can, Talk Realistically— not Judgmentally—about Consequences

Once you've introduced the A-B-C-D process to your girl, you may need to offer *tactful and nonjudgmental* support and guidance during the critical third and fourth stages as she practices the technique with you the first few times. Ask her why she wants to pursue a certain course of action. You may hear something like, "It felt good last time," or "I need to know what it's like," or "I want to have it." Without attacking, talk about how feelings like that result in actions—and actions result in consequences that your girl may not really want to go through.

Your aim here is to share stories from your own past or that of a friend—stories that make it perfectly clear that actions undertaken impulsively can carry consequences. Think about a time from your own past when you learned, perhaps abruptly, that "just feeling like it" is not always the best justification. Or perhaps there's a friend or mutual acquaintance who made a spur-of-the-moment decision that haunted her for the rest of her life. When has just doing "what I felt like doing"—as opposed to stopping and evaluating possible outcomes—resulted in big problems, problems your girl will feel motivated to avoid?

Cara, who is now seventeen with two children, shared her story with me:

"I got pregnant the first time I had sex. I was fourteen and really believed everything he said. He told me how he loved me. How I was the most beautiful girl he had ever seen. It felt so good to hear the words; my dad died when I was seven and my mom worked two jobs to support our family. She had my two younger brothers to watch. I was a good student. I really liked school. But I think I found myself wanting to be held and loved by someone. And there he was, holding me and listening to me. I felt loved.

"I really had no clue what he was doing. I only knew what he was saying. I only knew that it felt right. By the time I felt that we had gone too far, I didn't want to seem like a little girl, like I wanted time to stop. I didn't want him to go away and leave me because I was a baby. I was scared he wouldn't love me anymore. And that's how it happened.

"I didn't know that I was pregnant; my gym teacher actually spoke to me after she noticed I was getting bigger. I was so scared and ashamed. I ran away from home and my mom, left her with no idea about where I was. I just couldn't tell her. So I left that life completely.

"He didn't want anything to do with me. His mom found out; she let me stay with her. He felt that since I was with his mom that, well, I was his. After the baby was born, his mom took care of the baby. He started talking to me, telling me again how he loved me. Once again I fell for it, and I got pregnant again. I finally left and went back to my mom's house. She was shocked. She covered me with kisses; she had been so worried. I didn't know what else to do. Now I'm in the

teen mom program and learning how to grow up. I wish I hadn't acted so quickly, without thinking. I left my life—the life I had. I'll never get it back. I'm paying for my mistakes now."

By sharing such stories and asking supportive, but incisive questions (like "What do you think would happen then?"), you'll be helping your girl move away from an impulsive decision-making process—and toward an evaluative one that takes emotions into account, but also considers things like current circumstances, emerging moral values, likely outcomes, intuition, the experience of those whom we respect deeply, and our own long-term goals. Impulsive decision-making is highly susceptible to peer pressure. Evaluative decision-making is much more likely to help your girl base her decisions on factors that will support her in the long term.

Finally, you'll want to follow...

Rule Four: Encourage Her to Keep a Journal

If you can, take the time to write silently together—you in your own journal, and your girl in hers. This is a great bonding experience. If your girl doesn't have a journal, buy her one, and set aside a half hour with her to help her break it in!

Here are some superior journal questions you can use to help your girl break through "writer's block" and start writing about her own emotions. Encourage her to take at least ten minutes of continuous writing to answer them in her book—to her own satisfaction and in her own words.

- What am I grateful for in my life?

- What have I read recently that made a difference in my life? (If the answer is "Nothing," sit down and read passages of *The Diary of Anne Frank* to one another.)

- Who are the women in my family I admire most?

- What do I want to change in my life?

- What do I want to keep the same in my life?

- If I were to write a letter to someone who hurt me in the past—a letter I would never send—what would that letter say?

- If I knew that there would be no repercussions, no arguments, nor any discussions, what would I tell my parents?

- How would I finish these sentences? "The most difficult moment of my life was..." "If I could go back and change any of my actions, I'd..."

- What do I do that makes my own day difficult?

- If I were being given an award today, what would it be, and what would my (best friend/mother/next door neighbor/teacher) say about me in public before handing it over?

- What will I be like when I'm forty years old?

Writing about her own world enables your girl to explore thoughts, feelings, and perceptions safely and privately. It also enables her to come to terms with the emotional surges she encounters, to learn how intuition differs from following the dictates of a sudden (and fleeting) emotional reaction, and to share feelings with you about what she's written. Although you can feel free to share your own comments about your journal writings, you should *always* respect your own girl's privacy on this score. If she feels like talking about what she's written, she will; if she doesn't, she won't. Don't try to pressure her into sharing the contents of her journal with you, and for heaven's sake don't sneak unauthorized peeks—or encourage anyone else (including the girl's mother) to do so.

And speaking of confidentiality issues...

Suppose Your Girl Shares a Bombshell with You?

Reaching out to your girl in the way I'm describing in this chapter is likely to build a powerful emotional bond between the two of you—a bond that may make you feel conflicted if your girl decides (as she probably will) to share something with you that she trusts you will not tell her parents. It's all very well if that "something" has to do with run-of-the-mill confidences—the friends she's spending time with, the school she wants to attend, the minor grievances she has about her home life. But what do you do when your girl opens up to you emotionally and shares a major problem or lifestyle choice that you suspect her parents would want to know about?

This is one of the most difficult of all the challenges a mentor can face. Fortunately, the stance you need to take is fairly straightforward, although executing it can be a real test of your persistence, your commitment, and your integrity. If your girl shares a confidence with you—about pregnancy, about sexual activity, about drug use, or about another issue you know is in deep conflict with her parents' values—you *must* expand the focus of your discussions. You can still be supportive, you can still help her make decisions, you can still point the way to resources that will help her evaluate her situation. But you must always bring the discussion back to the essential questions:

- "How can you and I work together to bring your mother/father into this discussion?"

- "What is the worst thing your parents would do if you told them?"

- "Why do you think your parents would feel upset?"

- "Why do they look at this issue the way they do? How do you feel about that?"

- "If you didn't tell them, what consequences would you have to face?"

Use questions like these to help your girl look at the long-term guilt and trust issues she faces. Remember that the question of approaching your girl's parents can be presented in a hundred different ways. (It may well have to be if your girl is eager to keep her parents from learning about what's going on in her life.)

As much as your girl may want your support when it comes to keeping her parents uninformed about problems that could be seriously damaging to her, you *cannot* offer her that support. You are the adult; you have the wisdom and perspective necessary to look to the long term. You know about the difficulties and dilemmas she may encounter but may not yet be aware of. As a result, you'll want to act in her best interests; and sometimes, that means taking stands she won't like.

To maintain silence on issues you know are important to the girl's parents—or, even worse, to try to replace her parents or second-guess their judgment in critical areas—is a catastrophic mistake. You cannot replace your girl's parents, so don't try. Do anything and everything necessary to get serious (read: potentially damaging) problems onto the girl's parents' "radar screen."

Remember: You are in her life for a relatively short time. Her parents are her parents forever. How she deals with them and how she deals with her own emotional conflicts regarding them can have effects that last a lifetime. Don't make the mistake of assuming that your girl's versions of events in relationships with others are completely, or even substantially, accurate. She's probably still learning about what honesty in an adult relationship means. Step back and ask yourself, "If I were a parent, would I want to know about the problem this girl is facing?"

So, if involving the parents means a marathon mentoring session with you while you cajole, plead, explain, or tell stories from your own background, so be it. If involving the parents means constant telephone calls from you, so be it. If involving the parents means showing up at your girl's school to have an "ambush" lunch with her in a nearby cafe or restaurant where you can make your case yet again, so be it. If involving the parents means demonstrating, in graphic terms, how horrible the situation could get if it's ignored—and how much the girl's parents could do to help bring about a positive outcome—so be it. If involving the parents means threatening to show up for dinner at her house and bring the matter up while you, the girl, and her parents are all in attendance, so be it.

Your girl should not have to deal with the most difficult issues without giving her parents an opportunity to support her. Whatever faith, trust, and respect you've established in this relationship thus far, use it now. Make it clear to your girl that she has an obligation to inform her parents about the problems she's facing—and that you're not going to let the matter rest until she acts on that obligation. If and only if the parents then act irresponsibly, abusively, or insensitively, then you can start to take a more active role in the girl's decision-making process.

The Big Seven

Here's a table you can use to help you plot your strategy in seven "crisis areas" that may come to your attention once your girl has opened up to you emotionally. Don't panic—follow the steps laid out on the chart, and remember that not *every* conflict with the girl's family's values requires you to "appeal to the top." Some of these value conflicts, however, definitely do represent major crises in your girl's life and should be addressed in concert with her parents.

Please note: Your responsibilities as a mentor will be shaped by the environment within which you're working. If you're providing support as a teacher, scout leader, or as a member of some other organized group, you'll want to review your organization's policies and protocols for handling each of the situations discussed in the table at the end of the chapter.

A cautionary note is also in order about deep psychological and emotional problems, which do not appear on the list below. There is no simple solution to problems in this area. If, however, your girl talks openly about suicide or strong feelings of depression, that's almost certainly a sign that she's asking you for help in combatting the emotional challenges that frighten her, so get her in touch with a qualified professional as soon as possible. By the same token, if your girl shows sudden, dramatic and inexplicable shifts in her personality; or gives away treasured belongings; or begins to talk or write at length to you or others as though she were preparing to travel to a distant and unfamiliar place, she may be at risk for suicide in the very near future. She should not be left alone, and should immediately be put in touch with a qualified counselor or therapist. Check your phone directory for the number of the nearest suicide hotline; take care of your girl first, and then check in with parents and family members.

An Essential Role

By opening up to you emotionally, your girl will learn to trust you as someone who can be counted on to offer moral support when she makes a mistake. That's an important process to support—it means she's learning to reach out to grownups for support. At the same time, however, your girl also has to learn that taking care of herself is vitally important—even more important, in some situations, than avoiding the censure of her parents or saving her family from the embarrassment she may associate with her mistake. Although some of the situations you face together may be challenging, your commitment to her long-term well being will see you both through.

The earlier you begin to introduce yourself as a model for emotional self-management, the better off your girl will be. It's true that it takes a great deal of work over a fairly long period of time to help a girl develop the emotional mastery she needs to become a healthy adult. But it's also true that it takes *ten* times as much work to pull through the life problems she'll face if she learns the principles of emotional mastery too late!

Event	Why It May Be Happening	Steps Mentor Should Take
Smoking	Peer pressure; desire to be cool and fit in socially. Ages 10–16 are particularly vulnerable; these are the ages when most smokers get started on long-term smoking habits.	• If you smoke, stop smoking. • If members of your girl's family smoke, or if her parents have made the choice to permit her to smoke because they consider it a "minor vice," getting the girl to stop may be difficult. • Show your girl how awful cigarette smoke smells; put a bunch of old cigarettes in a jar, then ask the girl to smell it and explain that that's how her breath smells or will smell. • Ask your dentist for pictures that will show her how ugly cigarette-stained teeth look. Consider asking your mate or a male friend to talk about how unattractive women who smoke are. • Don't accommodate her smoking; if you're going to a restaurant, for example, don't sit in a smoking section. Explain that second-hand smoke is bad for the people around your girl—including you. • Accept that, in some cases, all you will be able to do is set appropriate personal limits and model a healthy lifestyle.

Event	Why It May Be Happening	Steps Mentor Should Take
Suspected Molestation by Father, Uncle, Teacher, Local Store-owner, etc.	90% of molestation occurs during contact with family members or close acquaintances of the family. Adults molest children because it gives them a sense of power and control. Molesters are usually themselves victims of child molestation and incest. Children and teenagers may find it difficult or impossible to speak up, especially when the molester is a family member or close friend. Despite the fact that they're innocent victims, they are afraid of being accused of causing the problem, or of "rocking the boat."	• Listen to your girl and record all the pertinent details. Remember that children very rarely lie about incestuous relationships or molestation. It's far more likely that the decision to speak is a sign of considerable courage and has arisen only after a long period of soul-searching. Remain calm, be receptive, comfort her, and encourage her to share her feelings and observations. • Notify her parents. If the father is identified as the molester, approach the mother one-on-one. You are your girl's representative in this situation and are morally obligated to act in her best interests. You must take action to try to keep your girl from being subjected to further abuse. • If the mother, or parents, do not take protective action, then you must intervene and notify the authorities. Call your state's toll-free child abuse hotline.

EVENT	WHY IT MAY BE HAPPENING	STEPS MENTOR SHOULD TAKE
Suspected Alcohol Abuse	Girls are drinking at earlier and earlier ages; their metabolism absorbs alcohol at a faster rate than boys'. In addition to the potential for lifelong problems associated with alcohol abuse, girls who drink face disastrous consequences during their youth and adolescence: unprotected sex, social gatherings where no one observes the "designated driver" rule, and the acceptance of violent behavior and abuse.	• Make sure you are modeling appropriate behavior. • Contact your local chapter of SADD (Students Against Drunk Driving) or Teen Al-Anon. These organizations are a great resource for your girl. • Show her the materials these organizations will provide; walk through the (many) reasons drinking is dangerous. • If you are convinced your girl has a real problem with alcohol, you will need to find a way to help her raise the issue with her parents and develop a strategy for recovery.

Event	Why It May Be Happening	Steps Mentor Should Take
Conflicts with Parents over Future Plans/Pessimism over Educational Prospects	She may have a low opinion of her own academic or survival capabilities. She may be receiving pressure from parents to pursue a career track for which she now feels unprepared. Studies indicate that girls are less likely to take advanced math and science programs, less likely to be directed to educational career tracks that lead to higher earning potential, and less likely to be called on in the classroom. Many media stereotypes equate intelligence in female characters with "bitchiness" (and solitude)—and portray ideal females as submissive or helpless ingenue figures who are not capable of "saving" themselves and who need the assistance of a man to do so.	• Contact nearby women's colleges and arrange trips with your girl. • Browse the Internet with your girl; focus in on educational institutions of interest to her. • Contact the local school district's career liaison or equivalent office; ask about girl-centered career programs, especially those that focus in on nontraditional careers.
Conflicts with Parents over Girl's Friends	Parents and teens often clash over their choice of friends; sometimes there is legitimate concern over the values social groups will promote; sometimes parents simply want children to associate with a "higher" or "better" class of friends. Parents may attempt to impose rules meant to protect their children, but these rules usually don't promote the formation of real-world coping skills.	• Invite her friends over to your place, then make your own assessment of the situation. • Tactfully offer your honest assessment of the girl's parents' concerns; if you believe there is potential for a problem at some point, tell her so in private. • Prepare to have the "My mom/dad is so unfair..." conversation over and over again. Listen attentively at all times.

EVENT	WHY IT MAY BE HAPPENING	STEPS MENTOR SHOULD TAKE
Girl Feels Her Privacy Is Violated	Girls need to know they have a safe space where they can sort things out, express emotions, and experience solitude. Many parents experience this need for privacy as deviousness or a desire to "keep secrets." ("About what?" parents wonder.) Conflicts may be frequent and intense.	• Help your girl identify the things she may be doing that could be perceived as hostile, dangerous, or secretive. If she is sneaking out at night, going out with friends who are radically different from her usual crowd, or displaying real changes of personality toward her parents, you may be able to help her understand how these behaviors are contributing to problems at home. Help her modify her behavior so that she can regain her parents' trust.
		• If necessary, help your girl create coping skills for privacy. She can go to the library for personal quiet time, keep a journal (and keep it in her school locker if she wishes), and perhaps spend quiet time at your place.
		• Some limit-testing is unavoidable (and essential). You will have to evaluate for yourself whether the conflicts are developmental (parents and teens dealing with classic independence issues) or if there are reasons to suspect serious breaches of trust that reflect problems that could be dangerous to your girl. If the latter is the case, you will probably want to work with your girl to re-establish healthy communication with her parents.

EVENT	WHY IT MAY BE HAPPENING	STEPS MENTOR SHOULD TAKE
Suspected Eating Disorder	Ultimate causes of bulimia (binging and purging through vomiting in order to maintain body weight) anorexia (prolonged self-starvation accompanied by a potentially fatal fixation on weight loss), and compulsive overeating (consumption of much larger quantities of food than are necessary for healthy weight maintenance) are complex and not yet completely understood. All three are psychological and biological disorders; all three may be accompanied by severe feelings of failure and self-loathing.	• If you strongly suspect or have first-hand knowledge of a problem—purposeful vomiting, reliance on weight-reduction pills when there is no significant difficulty with excess weight, or complete loss of appetite—your girl needs help, and quickly. You must see that your girl receives qualified professional help. A visit with her physician or a qualified therapist is a good short-term goal. • Encourage your girl to talk to her parents about the problem; if she is hesitant to do this, you should probably bring the issue up while you are in the room with the girl and her parents. (Informing your girl of your intention to do this may help her focus in on the importance of the problem.) This is not a secret to be kept. Often, when a problem like this is brought to the attention of parents, they will take strong and swift action to bring a qualified professional into the picture. • Never forget: Eating disorders are potentially lethal and *must not* be ignored.

7

The Fourth Essential: Spiritual Development

Spirituality is a complex subject, one that defies easy summary and often leads to disagreement among well-meaning people. I believe, however, that some form of spiritual progress, supported by a mentor, is essential to our daughters' journey out of girlhood and toward maturity. I also believe that just about any external disagreements (between you and a girl's parents, say) over the nature or form of spiritual growth can be overcome by focusing on one single, accessible aspect of the question.

Before we look at that "equal-opportunity" entry point for support of spiritual development, however, I want to examine an issue that is all too often ignored in discussions of adolescent development. In my experience as a counselor, I've found that it's very difficult for a girl to grow in a healthy way without *some* form of support for her interior spiritual life. Whatever name is attached to it, support for spiritual growth is essential for most young people. I've noticed, time and time again, that if this need is not addressed on some level, bad things tend to happen. Spirituality, in my view, is not an optional area of concern or an occasional subject to be considered once other, more pressing matters have been addressed. Whether or not spirituality is expressed through regular observance within an established religious tradition, it can and should emerge as a source of strength and balance for girls and young women.

In the struggle to find meaning and purpose within their lives, our daughters will develop their own answers to the important questions that arise in their lives. My own experience is that girls who do so, knowing in their hearts that there is a higher power to guide them, will be far more likely to come up with constructive answers than girls who receive little or no support in their spiritual lives.

I've met many, many kids who have come from family environments with serious problems—homelessness, drug abuse, physical abuse, alcoholism, you name it. I have yet to meet a child who encountered those kinds of problems, and who also cultivated a meaningful spiritual life—thanks to the guidance of a supportive mentor—who failed to develop appropriate strategies for coping with the challenges she faced.

Girls who receive support in their spiritual growth learn to develop their own working belief systems. They have a strong sense of self-worth. They have a sense of belief in themselves. They are better equipped to face—and make—decisions. They're more willing to take stands that are unpopular with peers and friends—but right for them. They're better equipped to develop their own appreciation of what's right and wrong. They're more willing to stand their ground and to make choices that will heighten their own sense of self-worth. And even if they experience problems at home, they're in a better position to deal with the challenges that come their way without losing sight of their own goals and values.

Girls who *don't* receive support in their spiritual development, however, face a much more difficult path. Without a spiritual identity, one that's right for them and of their own choosing, girls often find it difficult to confront the risks that are part and parcel of young adult life today. They don't develop belief systems that make sense for their own lives and their sense of self-worth often suffers. In a vain attempt to search out deeper meanings in their lives, they often end up making choices that retard their own growth and leave them feeling less fulfilled than ever. That's a potentially dangerous cycle.

Some years back, Bob Dylan wrote a song called "Gotta Serve Somebody," in which he argued that spiritual energies have to be pointed in some direction, either constructive or destructive, but that they can't be ignored. The principle is worth remembering for anyone—mentor, parent, or religious instructor—who seeks to bring about positive change in a girl's life.

The Attitude of Gratitude

The best and simplest way to help your girl make spiritual growth a reality in her own life is to help her develop a "gratitude instinct" that eventually becomes second nature to her.

In order to do this, of course, you will need to learn to model that behavior—and cultivate an attitude of gratitude in your own life. This is a lifelong endeavor, of course, and the fact that your role as a mentor necessitates a conscious effort to bring gratitude into your life in a conscious way is one of the significant side benefits of reaching out to help any young girl.

Gratitude is nonsectarian. Even people who can't make sense of how "spirituality" fits into their lives can learn to embrace the idea of gratitude and benefit from it. So use gratitude as the cornerstone of your efforts to nurture your girl's internal growth.

My Aunt Lu helped me to learn that one of the most powerful resources at my disposal is the ability to find and celebrate the blessings God had bestowed on me. To a teenager who was feeling as isolated, withdrawn, and confused as I was, it took work—and constant reinforcement—for me to learn to be thankful for the simplest things in my life. I still have journal entries in which I struggle to find things to be thankful for, entries that settle on simple things—my dog, the fact that there was electricity in the house, the evening meal, the books in my room, the roof over my head—and celebrate all of them as God's gifts.

Nowadays, I think those journal entries are some of the most important motivators of my decision to emerge from a cocoon that might well have smothered me. Explicitly giving thanks for "the basics," the things we usually take for granted, is one of the very best ways to deepen one's spiritual life. Modeling this behavior is one of the very best ways mentors can help their girls grow spiritually.

Ten Things You Can Do to Help Reinforce a Perspective of Gratitude in Your Girl's Life

1. Ask your girl, "What one thing are you grateful for right now, in this moment?" (Offer thanks for your own "present-tense gift" first. Developing an attitude of present-tense gratitude takes practice, so do some thinking yourself before you launch this question. You might let your girl know that you're grateful for the opportunity to spend time with her; or for your husband's support during a recent problem at home; or for the gift of laughter you experienced when something amusing broke the tension at work.)

2. Show her a written list of ten things for which you yourself are deeply grateful. (Don't write at length about how much you love, for instance, your new swimming pool; instead, focus on the people, relationships, and easily overlooked day-to-day gifts that reinforce your sense of having been given a special mission on earth. You might choose to include your relationship with the girl herself on the list.)

3. Suggest that you each think of, and then discuss, one recent experience that makes you feel hopeful about the future. (These types of discussions can be very powerful motivators; offer to go first.)

4. Ask your girl what she most enjoys about a religious system of interest to her and whether or not that system is one her parents embrace. (Remember that adolescence is a time of experimentation and examination; unless the religious discipline under discussion is patently manipulative, abusive, or otherwise in conflict with your girl's best interests, let her explore what she finds most exciting about the discipline that interests her. If *no* religious ideas or structures appear to hold interest for her, you might consider a trip to the library, or a session on the Internet, to explore the religious heritage of the girl's family.)★

5. Talk about family members who have had a positive impact on your lives. (You might, for instance, talk about the many reasons you have to be grateful for your own mother and father—and use that discussion to move into an examination of the specific ways your girl's own parents have helped and supported her.)

★   Although you may choose to adopt a more open-minded attitude toward new forms of religious and spiritual expression than the girl's parents, you should make a point of avoiding anything that might conceivably be viewed as an attack on the family's existing faith. That means that you probably should not encourage or suggest participation in specific new avenues of religious or spiritual exploration, even ones that have nothing to do with your own faith. Listening supportively to a teenage girl's questions about a new faith structure is one thing; taking action on your own to introduce her to a new mode of worship, one that differs from the tradition of her parents, is quite another.

6. Identify a close friend who almost always makes you feel good about yourself and the situations you face. Ask whether your girl has such a friend in her life. (If she does, help her to remember the times when that friend has stood by her and supported her, perhaps during hard times. If your girl *does not* have such a friend, ask her to think of a teacher or counselor who has helped make life a little easier.)

7. Spend some time on an activity you know that both of you enjoy; select the activity exclusively for its capacity to make both of you happy. Then, at the conclusion of your time there, join hands and make a mutual expression of thanks for the trip. (You might choose to visit a favorite museum, or spend time stitching together, or play a game you both enjoy.)

8. Volunteer. (Take an hour with your girl to help out at a local homeless shelter, nursing home, or fund-raising drive—and then, at the end of your work together, give thanks for the opportunity to make a difference in the lives of others. You may also want to express your gratitude for something that is present in your life and your girl's life—but absent in the lives of the people you are helping.)

9. Simply read to each other; then talk about what you most enjoyed in what you read. One of my favorite, can't-miss texts to share with older girls is the timeless classic *Little Women* by Louisa May Alcott.

Another option for younger girls is the *American Girl* ® book series.)

10. Explore a scene of natural beauty together. (Take some time together to quietly enjoy a park, forest, beach, mountaintop or river ... and do so long enough for both of you to appreciate the physical and emotional power of God's creation.)

That last item may be a particularly powerful one. A picnic lunch in a state park can be the perfect opportunity for both of you to realize how lucky you are to have the opportunity to see the miracle of the unfolding seasons. These trips help you help your girl to experience, first-hand, the reality of the processes of growth, decay, and new growth, and to understand that life goes on in an endless, ever-more-intricate dance.

By exposing ourselves, and our girls, to the unfolding processes of nature, we encounter that for which we must all be ultimately grateful: the gift of participation in the dance of life itself. By helping to open her eyes to the cycles of life visible in trees, in grass, in sea creatures, in animals, you can help her appreciate—and be grateful for—her own interconnectedness with the natural world. She may be used to thinking of herself as somehow separate from that world, just as the rest of us may be. But her sense of dawning wonder at the size and scope of the dance, and her thankfulness at being part of the ongoing miracle that is consciousness, are realities that you can help to bring about and benefit from in your own spiritual life.

Gratitude makes a difference! Gratitude for the workings of nature, for family members, for friends, for the gifts that make physical survival possible, for the gift of another chance with each new morning—each instance of genuine gratitude helps to support, reinforce, and extend your girl's emerging sense of self-worth. Gratitude helps girls understand that there is something deep within that guides them, nurtures them, and cares for them, regardless of what the world outside says. Gratitude reminds girls that, in the words of the spiritual classic *Desiderata*, they have a "right to be here." Gratitude helps them develop a sense of purpose, and provides the perspective they need to escape the trap of defining themselves exclusively through the perceptions of others. Gratitude helps girls encounter the inner self who sustains, provides, and nourishes them on countless levels; and gratitude reminds girls that their "deep self" is ready, willing, and able to serve as the guidepost to correct action, a guidepost that is far more reliable than any number of self-interested outsiders.

Once you are grateful, you acknowledge the existence of an entity worthy of gratitude, and, whether or not you are comfortable expressing it explicitly, you acknowledge your own fundamental dependence on that higher power. Gratitude is the act that makes spiritual awareness and growth possible, both for you and the girl you are mentoring.

By habitually and openly acknowledging that for which we are grateful, and encouraging our girls to do the same (either out loud, during informal one-on-one conversation, before meals, or on paper as a subject for journal writing), we help our girls to transcend virtually all that is potentially divisive or controversial about spiritual practice. We also help them to take full advantage of a good deal of that which is life-affirming and powerful within any spiritual tradition she may be pursuing.

I do not mean to suggest that the whole range of spiritual practice is simple, or easily summarized—but I do mean to suggest that virtually every religious tradition places a powerful emphasis on the idea of giving thanks for what we have received in our lives, and for acknowledging the role of a higher power in delivering that for which we are grateful. By serving as models for the active cultivation of gratitude in one's life—even (especially!) during times of trial—mentors can shine a spotlight on a component of spirituality that people of nearly all beliefs, and a fair number of people who reject any form of spiritual practice, can accept as worthwhile.

Don't get distracted by labels or dogma. Don't challenge the girl (or her family) to accept specific religious values that are, as a practical matter, more likely to exclude than they are to inspire. Don't worry about what to call things. Instead, simply focus on what you're grateful for in your own life—and help your girl to do the same.

The Anti-Gratitude Machine

The dictionary tells us that gratitude is "the quality or feeling of being grateful or thankful." I think that's true as far as it goes, but I also believe that true gratitude carries with it an underlying sense of purpose that is hard to define through words alone. When we're truly grateful—for food or shelter, for the love of a family member, for the greatness of a poem that moves us, for the support of a friend when we're dealing with problems in our lives—then we acknowledge, on some level, that we are blessed—and that there is, by extension, some reason for our having been blessed. We feel ourselves more a part of "the grand design of things" when we are grateful on a deep level, at the level of the heart. Unfortunately, thanks to a relatively recent technological innovation, most of us receive several hours a day of highly sophisticated hypnotic suggestion designed to render us as *ungrateful* as possible in both the short and long terms.

For better or for worse (and often, I think, for both at the same time), the consumer culture in which we live requires a massive, continually reinforced desire to possess things on the part of millions upon millions of people. It's hard to desire more when you are fundamentally satisfied with what you have, so some strategy for instilling desire is necessary. The primary technology by which that desire is spread far and wide is, you guessed it, the television sets you and I watch every day. (I say "sets" because so many households these days have more than one.) I don't think television is evil, but I do think the way it's used in our culture is troubling for those who take as their goal the development of an environment that supports sustained spiritual growth. It's my experience—and the experience of many others with whom I've worked over the years—that this "anti-gratitude machine" degrades our ability to be thankful to a higher power, or to virtually anyone else, for that which is good in our lives.

Most television programming robs us of the ability to cultivate gratitude with charming (and ruthless) efficiency. It may be unrealistic—or even unpatriotic—to suppose we can eliminate this instrument's influence in our lives and the lives of our daughters. But it is certainly essential to spiritual growth that we keep it from becoming the sole or primary influence on the way we and our girls look at the many gifts of life, or from persuading us not to look at those gifts at all. To put the matter bluntly, life without gratitude is life without a sense of purpose—and life totally immersed in commercial television is life essentially devoid of gratitude.

That may seem a heavy charge to lay against a machine that provides us with entertainment, news, and, yes, education, but I'm convinced that it's a fair charge, and one worth examining in some detail, given the alarming negative effect television has had on spiritual development in our society—not only in the lives of girls and young women, but in the lives of the vast majority of people.

Every eight to ten minutes (at least), commercial television quite literally hypnotizes its viewers. By that I mean that it distracts us with words or images, appeals to our strongest emotional or physical responses, encourages us to relax conscious evaluative tools, and passes along post-hypnotic suggestions, most of which are meant to make us associate a powerful positive feeling—or the absence of a negative feeling—with the purchase of a product or service.

Commercial television aims to convince us, at a very deep level, that we need what we haven't yet got.*

Sound spiritual growth, on the other hand, requires us to accept, at a very deep level, that we have what we need and are cared for by a higher power. The most famous Psalm of all *doesn't* say, "The Lord is usually my shepherd; most of the time I find that I don't experience want." Instead, it transforms the mind of the reader or speaker or singer by speaking of present care and future support in the same breath: "The Lord is my shepherd, I shall not want."

These two primary messages—that of commercial television and that of healthy spiritual practice—are fundamentally incompatible. Because of that, I believe that it's impossible to be a good mentor for your girl if a television is usually (or frequently!) on during your interactions together. In the early going, while you're looking for ways to reach out to your girl, it may make sense to sit in on a soap opera or two, or to appeal to some television program that she has a strong interest in while you're trying to find common interests. Once your relationship is underway, however, it's important for you to serve as a bridge to a set of values utterly different from those promulgated by commercial television. You'll need to use the activities discussed earlier in this book— physical challenges, visits to places that represent new intel-

---

* Commercial television is certainly not the only medium of mass communication that propagates this message. Print advertisements, radio spots, and product placements in feature films encourage essentially the same outlook on life. I think it's fair to say, though, that television is perhaps the most effective and pervasive of all these media in reaching girls—and the rest of us—with "anti-gratitude" messages.

lectual worlds, activities like journal-keeping that encourage emotional discovery—to help ensure that your girl's time with you is television-free time.

By making sure the television is *off* when your girl comes to visit you, and by planning activities and expeditions that have nothing to do with the materialistic values forwarded by the often manipulative marketers who target young girls through television, you'll be taking a very important step indeed toward supporting your girl's spiritual growth.

You'll also be making it possible for you and your girl to share...

Moments of Silence

When I worked at a youth center, I always made a point of starting out sessions with "my girls" with a brief period of silence. I'd gather them all in a circle, ask them to close their eyes, and encourage them to breathe deeply. Then I'd stop talking for five, ten, or fifteen minutes, depending on what the girls were used to. The more experienced the girls, the longer I'd sit with them. Then, when it was time to move out of our silence, I'd talk about something I was grateful for in my life, and ask each girl in turn to talk about something for which she was grateful.

If you're looking for a way to bring an awareness of spirituality into your girl's life (and your own) in a powerful and immediate way, that's the recipe. It never failed to leave each and every one of us feeling relaxed, refreshed, grounded, and connected to something larger than ourselves. The act of sitting with your girl—whether it's just the two of you, or a group of ten or twelve people—has a remarkable calming and centering effect. Rather than putting the labels of "prayer" or "meditation" on these sessions, I would simply experience them with my girls. These five or ten or fifteen minutes don't have to belong to any religious tradition. They don't have to be described as a "technique" meant to help the participants attain any particular goal. These minutes can be, if you like, absolutely nothing.

This particular brand of "nothing," however, has some remarkable advantages.

The Power of "Nothing"

This "nothing"—simply sitting quietly in a chair for a few moments, breathing deeply, and then talking about what you're grateful for—is, I believe, the only immediately practical, immediately accessible, immediately beneficial therapy for girls who are in deep crisis. This silent time together, I found, helped girls who had been beaten black and blue by violent boyfriends. It helped girls who had been harassed mercilessly by cruel boys in the halls of their high school. It helped girls who had been sexually abused by close family friends or relatives, including one girl who had been the object of her own father's sexual obsession.

Sitting quietly (and comfortably) together for an extended period, and then focusing on areas of our lives for which we could show gratitude, had a powerful galvanizing effect on each of us. It allowed us to tap into something more powerful than ourselves. It motivated us to make powerful positive changes in our lives. It pointed each and every one of us in the direction we needed to go and strengthened the bonds between each of us. Conflicts and interpersonal problems didn't exactly vanish as a result of my having chosen to begin each day with "my girls" in this way, but these difficulties were easier to put into the proper perspective after we'd gathered together for our "quiet circle."

Girls with the most extraordinary (and tragic) personal histories received the support they needed and took on renewed strength—from the group, yes, but from something deep within themselves as well. They began the long, difficult task of overcoming deep-seated feelings of abandonment and worthlessness, and I don't believe they could have motivated themselves to do so in quite the same purposeful way had we not taken the time to sit together.

Please note that the tool I used—silent time, followed by spoken gratitude—is *not* to be confused with proselytizing or guilt-mongering. Avoid, at all costs...

- Lecturing your girl about the obligations imposed on her by her (or, even worse, your) religious system.

- Issuing dire warnings about the consequences of past or future actions.

- Reciting unsolicited scriptural passages for your girl's benefit.

- Offering specific advice based on your own religious convictions, or on your own interpretation of religious texts.

- Appealing to the example of other people (particularly siblings) who have stronger religious inclinations than your girl does.

Your relationship with your girl may grow to incorporate a specific sectarian religious dimension—but in most cases that's for her to initiate, not you. The mentor's job is to offer silent support during the quiet time I'm proposing, and then to put the emphasis on spoken expressions of gratitude. This invaluable session of silence and brief spoken thanks, which works effectively in a one-on-one setting as well as in groups, is an essential feature of a successful mentoring relationship. I strongly suggest that you find some way to work it into your time with your girl once you have established a basic level of trust and mutual respect.

If your girl shows signs of skepticism or hostility when you ask her to sit quietly with you for a few minutes, don't issue demands or ultimatums. Explain that daily quiet time is part of your own routine. (If it isn't, make it so!) At the outset of the relationship, you may choose to move directly into the "gratitude" element of the session by asking your girl questions like the following:

- What was the most difficult thing that happened to you in the past (week/month/year)? What do you think you were supposed to learn from this? How can someone make an experience like that meaningful?

- If you could talk to God right now, what would you say?

- What would you most like to accomplish in your life?

- Why do you think God put us here?

- When you think back over your life, what's the one event you're most thankful for?

Your Own Growing Faith

It should go without saying that all the earnest pronouncements about gratitude in the world will count for very little in your girl's life if she perceives your own spiritual life as narrow and incomplete. I would submit that part of the challenge of serving as a mentor for any girl or young woman is to make a serious commitment to living a faith-based life—a life based, in a fundamental way, on connection to an entity more powerful than you are, however you define that power. Once again, it's not your responsibility to develop a perfect model of behavior, but to demonstrate for your girl how an actual human being, complete with doubts, lapses, and frailties, conducts an ongoing relationship with the higher power.

Can you be an atheist and a mentor at the same time? Probably, but my own experience is that it's unlikely that a mentor with no spiritual life whatsoever is going to be in a position to support her girl fully. In other words, if you can't serve as this person's spiritual model, you owe it to your girl to help her find someone who can.

I do think there's a time and place for telling your girl exactly how your spiritual life has helped you in the past. Ellen Marie, a close friend of mine and a nationally-acclaimed professional speaker, has ongoing mentor relationships with many of the girls who have attended her extraordinary presentations. She's always been very forthcoming about sharing stories with them, stories that illustrate how her faith in God—her sense that God had a specific mission for her—helped her make the right choices during her teenage years. Ellen Marie has no hesitation about telling her girls about times when she had the opportunity to experiment sexually and chose not to. Ellen Marie's enduring sense of purpose helped her then, at a time when most of her friends were sexually active.

Although many of her friends (and any number of boys) pressured her to follow their supposedly "cool" example, her strong spiritual background had left her with a conviction that sex should be celebrated as part of a sanctified marriage commitment. The specifics of her denomination's religious beliefs, which supported Ellen Marie's decision, weren't as important to her girls as the decision itself and the life she's lived in the years since. They could tell that Ellen Marie's choices had been guided, not by the pressures of peers, but by a powerful sense of purpose grounded in personal faith.

That same sense of purpose, the heart-certain sense of being placed on earth for a reason, helps Ellen Marie to reach out to girls today and share the events and choices in her life in terms that will make sense to them. She is, for me, a perfect example of a mentor who is able to communicate constructive faith-based values to her girls. She shares with her girls exactly how the choice to follow her faith has given her the freedom to celebrate who she is and develop all aspects of herself—regardless of what others may think of her choices.

Rage and Meaning

I've seen young women decide, in an instant, to take charge of their lives because they found a sense of peace in accepting that they could not expect to control everything that would happen to them. Under the influence of an effective mentor who knows how to listen and knows how to pose effective questions, these girls learned to "let go and let God." They learned to accept that there are some difficulties that God sends our way that are hard to understand at the time but have the effect of strengthening us for future trials or helping us to help others in ways we never would have thought possible.

I've also seen girls respond to periods of trial and pain by venting—by giving in to tempests of blind rage that have, at their core, difficult questions like:

- If there is a God, how could God allow something like this to happen to me?

- What makes you think doing what you say will help me?

- Why should I believe you?

- Why should I believe anyone?

- Why would I believe in God?

In addressing spiritual development issues, I've dealt with many furious young women over the years, and I've come away with two key lessons.

The first is that, when someone is angry, it doesn't do much good to try to convince her that she isn't angry. Even if your girl is saying things that shock you, even if she's attacking your church or your own belief system, even if she's raising questions that you feel powerless to address, you have to avoid the temptation to try to talk your way out of experiencing this situation. Rage at God, or at religious systems, or at you, is better than no feeling at all. Rage means your girl still cares enough to express herself about the issues you're raising. Remain hooked in, don't challenge her, and listen to what she has to say. Don't ask that she deny her anger. You must both acknowledge what has happened to her.

The second big lesson is that even tragic experiences can be imparted with a sense of meaning. Girls with whom I've worked have survived truly horrific ordeals—including rape, physical assault, and emotional abuse of exceptional cruelty—by asking themselves, or by being asked, questions like the following:

- How can I use what happened to me to help other people?

- What lessons have I drawn from this experience?

- How can the lessons I've learned from this experience make me stronger?

- What can I do to help make sure that another girl doesn't go through what I had to go through?

- What can I do to reach out to people who faced the same challenges I faced?

Although they have no explicit spiritual content, questions like the ones I've just posed do have a tendency to help girls in crisis to attach meaning to experiences that seem fundamentally meaningless, and to help them move from rage to a sense of purpose—or even divinely inspired mission—in their lives.

Share your own darkest moments with your girl. Explain how and when and why you came to believe that there was a reason for the difficulties you faced. In my case, for instance, despite—or perhaps because of—what I perceived as betrayals on the part of my father and my uncle, I learned and grew. I experienced a great deal of pain, but even so, I was able to develop and appeal to new strengths within myself, to center myself and bring myself in contact with a higher power when things seemed overwhelming (which still happens pretty regularly, by the way), and, eventually, to reach out to hundreds of girls. I learned how to teach them some of the things I'd learned about navigating the difficult path from girlhood and adolescence to young adulthood.

My experiences turned out to have had a reason—a reason I consciously bestowed on them. They occurred so that I could make a difference in the lives of other people. I've shared that remarkable transition with hundreds of girls over the years, and it usually earns a measure of respect and admiration from even the toughest cases. Girls want to know—"How did you do it? How did you manage to make sense of the problems you faced?" And I'm happy to talk about that and about the spiritual dimension of that transition.

I explain to them that I had to make my way through a whole series of challenges, including my own assumptions that a) life should always make sense on my terms, and b) I was entitled to have complete control over my own surroundings at all times. My personal experiences with abandonment and sexual abuse pretty much destroyed those two ideas, but in time I was able to develop a spiritual life that has allowed me to celebrate the many, many gifts that God has chosen to bestow on me, including a few experiences that certainly didn't *feel* like gifts at the time, but that I could not deny had helped me to identify a deep and abiding sense of purpose in my life.

Nowadays, I can tell my girls that, in what seemed like the darkest possible moments, I eventually found myself reaching out to God and accepting that some challenges were beyond my understanding or control. Another way of looking at the process sounds like this: I passed through a period of insecurity, fear, and anger, and eventually found myself accepting the notion of surrender to God's will. I was fortunate to have strong women around me who supported that choice, who had rich spiritual lives of their own, and who knew how to listen to me supportively during my most painful times.

That's what good mentors do. They model the behavior their girls need to see, and help make the later transitions possible. I believe this cycle is just as crucial in the spiritual realm as it is in any of the other four essential areas.

All the same, mentors must remember that it's impossible to *impart* a spiritual breakthrough to another person. These stages must be experienced on their own terms, and at your girl's own schedule. Sometimes it takes a while to move from rage to surrender. Sometimes it doesn't. Whatever rate of spiritual development emerges as the right one for your girl, as her mentor, you must respect and support her own unique progression. You can't, as the old saying goes, rip the skin off the snake. And you certainly shouldn't try to judge a girl's spiritual progress by her ability to rephrase your own deeply held religious beliefs. A better yardstick is her emerging sense of purpose, of being placed on this earth for a particular reason—unique, incontestable, and intuitively right.

Five More Ways to Help Deepen Your Girl's Spiritual Life

In addition to encouraging her to experience and enhance an "attitude of gratitude" in her life, turn off the television during your time together, and share moments of silence with you, your girl can support her emerging spiritual identity in a variety of ways. Help her by pursuing the following steps.

1. Work with her to develop affirmations that are appropriate for her situation. (Encourage her to use her journal writing as an opportunity to repeat affirmations in written form: "God has a plan for me, and I am living out that plan in my every movement and every action." Other affirmations you might want to consider introducing include: "When I close my eyes I can reach for you and feel your love" and "Guide me in your light, show me the way so that my path brings me growth." If you're looking for a great book that will point you and your girl toward some spiritually powerful affirmations, check out *Designing a Woman's Life* by Judith Couchman, published by Multnomah in 1995, or any of the affirmation books produced by Hazelton Publishers.

2. Point her toward resources that will help her understand the other faiths about which she expresses curiosity. (Understand, too, that adolescence is a period of experimentation and trial; avoid the temptation to issue dire warnings as she examines the faiths and belief systems of other people. Remember that it is a very common pattern for girls to explore faiths outside their family's belief system and then return to that original belief system with renewed vigor and commitment.)

3. Tactfully encourage her to attend religious services within her own family's faith. (She can still read and learn about other disciplines, of course—but there's nothing wrong with helping her to re-establish contact with the faith system she grew up with. If she resists, however, you shouldn't press the issue. If you and your girl share the same religious beliefs, you may want to suggest that the two of you attend services together. Take this opportunity, if you can, to introduce your girl to a female religious officiant who has inspired you or made a difference in your life.)

4. Share stories about the ways your own spiritual development or religious beliefs have helped you to make the right choices in your life. (The closer the circumstances you've faced match the problems and challenges in your girl's life, the more likely you'll be to make an impact on her.)

5. Encourage your girl to join girls' and women's groups active within her religious tradition. (These groups might include women's choirs, charitable organizations, or prayer groups. In addition to reinforcing important support systems for her own spiritual growth, the social interaction she will experience as a result of taking part in such groups will be a big plus in her life. Remember, the goal is not to make your mentoring relationship with your girl the new center of her life—but to enable her to initiate and support new relationships with peers and adults.)

The Opposite of Fear

I believe that faith is the opposite of fear—and that God gives girls strength by enabling them to develop faith in themselves and in their appointed purpose on this earth. By accepting that there are a variety of different religions and faith systems, and by celebrating the many gifts God has bestowed on all of us, mentors can reach out to girls who are aching—as most are—to receive support on their spiritual journeys. They can help their girls learn that there are consequences, positive and negative, short-term and long-term, for every action. And they can deepen their own relationships with the higher power that animates and enriches and inspires all human life.

8

The Fifth Essential : Financial Accountability

essica, an elderly woman in my neighborhood, had never paid much attention to her financial affairs. Checking accounts, retirement decisions, mortgage payments, tax forms—she had a stock response for anyone who tried to talk to her about such matters. "Marty handles all that," she would answer, smiling. "He's a whiz with numbers, and I'm not. When it comes to handling money, I pass everything over to him."

That answer had served Jessica well enough for the forty-seven years of her marriage to Marty, who worked as an accountant for most of his life and was indeed very good with numbers. But four years ago Marty died, leaving Jessica—who had no children and no other close relatives—in charge of her own finances for the first time in her life. Deposits from Marty's pension made it into her bank account without too much difficulty, but she never did manage to make sense of the paperwork.

At the age of seventy-three, Jessica found herself receiving bank statements, insurance forms, and tax bills that she could no longer "pass over to Marty." If she'd had a larger support network—or been more inclined to reach out to some of her neighbors in the years following Marty's death—she might have been able to avoid the tragedy that followed, a tragedy that was all the more poignant because it was completely preventable.

Jessica simply ignored each and every one of the financial papers that came her way. She didn't call a relative to help her out, because there were no relatives to help her out—at least, none she considered close enough to call family. And she didn't call a financial counselor or other professional because she knew none. That was Marty's department, she told herself, and she didn't really know enough about money to make the right decisions or pick the right advisors.

So she did nothing.

Four years of complete neglect led to a huge wave of tax penalties—penalties that could easily have been avoided if Jessica had only found a way to make some sense of the notices that came her way from local, state, and federal authorities. She wasn't rich, but she could have handled her tax obligations with her income. What she couldn't handle, it turned out, was the staggering accumulation of penalties that accompanied her failure to file income tax returns and pay property-related tax assessments. By the time a neighbor was finally recruited to help her make some sense of the situation, Jessica was in well over her head. She owed huge sums in local, state, and federal taxes and charges. And she couldn't pay what she owed.

She had to sell her home, the home she'd lived in for half a century.

Jessica's inaction was motivated by fear and by the unspoken hope that financial choices would somehow take care of themselves if she pretended they didn't exist. Women of all ages simply can't afford such delusions when it comes to their finances—if only because they tend to outlive the men who marry them!

I make a habit of sharing Jessica's story with the young women I mentor, and it usually makes quite an impression. It gets them to focus in on the reality that they really are responsible for their own finances, and that failing to address important questions can have catastrophic results.

In this chapter, you'll look at the last of the "big five" areas where mentors can make a difference in the lives of their girls. Mentors must motivate their girls to assume control of their financial destinies—by, for instance, beginning savings plans during their early prime earning years, or by meeting with financial planners who can help them develop new goals and strategies.

The best way to encourage financial awareness, of course, is to lead by example and to share with your girl the many choices about money you must make in your own life. Maybe you're not an expert financial strategist—but you're an expert *you*, and that's what your girl needs to see most. You need to present yourself as a role model who approaches the issue of financial accountability in a very different manner than Jessica, and who is, as a result, likely to enjoy a different outcome in terms of the lifestyle you'll purse in your sixties, seventies, eighties, and beyond.

Most important of all, mentors must demonstrate, by personal example, that fear and denial are not constructive options for women facing important financial choices. If there are gaps in your financial planning skills and if there are places where you need to improve your own money management work, you and your girl will both benefit from your choice to acknowledge openly where improvements need to be made. Take action in a way she can see and understand.

This chapter isn't the last word on taking control of your own financial destiny—that's another book entirely. What this chapter will do, however, is give you some constructive ideas about specific ways you can engage girls in the real-world financial choices you yourself make. It will also pass along some fundamental ideas on career growth, credit, negotiation, and savings that can help your girl establish a strong foundation for financial planning in her own life.

Some of the specific advice that follows is geared toward your emerging relationship with older girls; but even girls in the nine-to-twelve age range can benefit from watching you put into action the basic principles of, for instance, savings and negotiation. (Actually, it's around the age of nine that specific, narrowly focused, financial issues—tracking down the cash for important future purchases—start to emerge as relevant topics for girls. It may be easier to hold your girl's attention on some of these issues than you think.)

The Ten Commandments of Sound Financial Management

Here are ten basic guidelines meant to be accessible to normal human beings, not financial experts. You can incorporate (or strengthen) all ten of them in your own life with a very minimal investment of time and effort. I suggest setting aside at least one Sunday a month as a time when you can focus on these issues.

As a woman, you should make sure that each of these ten steps is incorporated as part of your regular regime of financial self-analysis, a routine far too many women fail to build into their lives. As a mentor, you should make sure your girl understands the choices you've made in each of the ten areas.

Commandment I: Thou Shalt Take Control of Thy Checking Account, and Shalt in No Way Allow It to Control Thee. Both you and your girl should be comfortable with the practice of balancing a checkbook shortly after receiving each monthly statement. There are a great many software programs available today that make balancing one's checkbook remarkably easy. *Quicken* ® is probably the best. If you're already using such a program, turn it on and show your girl how it works. If you're not using a personal money management program, invest the minimal cash necessary to buy one, and take an afternoon to sit down at the computer with your girl and work through the onscreen tutorial together. (For information on purchasing *Quicken*, a truly extraordinary and, as advertised, easy-to-use financial management program, call 800-224-0517.)

- Go with your girl to the bank. Help her open a checking account or savings account.

Commandment II: Thou Shalt Set a Little Something Aside Every Month. The words "monthly savings plan" may sound boring and painfully pragmatic to your girl, so you probably shouldn't use them. Instead of thinking in terms of clichés like "saving for a rainy day," try to put the focus on times when you yourself experienced a serious financial setback—perhaps when you were a young woman just out of school—and had to go without something important. The moral: If you'd had a couple of month's salary saved up, you could have averted disaster. (We'll talk about some realistic savings strategies a little later on in this chapter.)

- Help your girl identify times when she may need money on an emergency basis. Perhaps her parents' car could get scratched while she's driving; she'd be held responsible for repairing the damage.

Commandment III: Thou Shalt Open an IRA. An individual retirement account (IRA) is a simple, easy to understand, virtually painless investment tool for those who won't be able to plan a secure retirement on Social Security income alone (and that's everyone). There are lots of different kinds of IRAs for you and your girl to learn about. They may not be the only investment you or your girl will ever need, but IRAs, which allow working people to contribute up to a maximum annual sum and defer tax on the interest until retirement, represent a great starting-place for the novice investor. Starting and contributing to an IRA is a safe, simple way to help maintain financial stability during one's retirement years. The earlier your girl starts, the better off she'll be. For more information on IRAs, talk to your local bank (or see Commandment IV).

- Be amazed! Ask your financial planner (see below) to work out how much money your girl would have by age sixty-five if she started saving twenty dollars a month now by putting it into an IRA.

Commandment IV: Thou Shalt Meet with a Responsible Financial Planner. Take the time to schedule a meeting with a CFP (Certified Financial Planner; for more information on how to contact a CFP who can help you, call the Institute of Certified Financial Planners at 718-236-7077). Make sure your girl accompanies you on this visit. Let her see exactly where your own knowledge gaps are and let her see that there's no crime in asking for help from an expert. Ask—whether for the first or the hundredth time—for an assessment of your overall financial situation, and get advice on the best ways for you to set up an investment plan that works for you.

- Call your financial institution and ask them to set up a financial seminar for girls (or, as they may prefer to think of them, future customers). Share the need for an early instructional program. Contact your associates, friends, and family, and encourage them to bring their girls to the event.

Commandment V: Thou Shalt Set Meaningful Financial Goals. After sitting down with a CFP and surveying the "lay of the land," you should be in a position to ask yourself some tough questions and to show your girl how you plan to go about answering them. What are the best investment vehicles for you? What mutual funds should you be looking at? How much do you want to have saved or invested two years from now? Five years from now? Twenty years from now? After your meeting with the CFP, sit down with your girl and ask her to spend some time working with you. You should each take a pen and a piece of paper and jot down your most important financial goals in both the short and long terms; and then start thinking about steps you can take this month to make those goals a reality. Swap lists and discuss each other's entries.

- Work up short- and long-term financial goals with your girl. Figure out how much it will cost to pay for the car she wants, the college she would like to go to, the roller blades she's dying to skate around town in, or that computer game she wants to play. Help her work out a savings plan to achieve the goal. (For my Girl Scout troop, we figured out how much we needed to save to go on our troop trip. Then we broke it down: How much could we make from cookie sales? How much additional money would we need to earn? Girls see the target, then they buy into it, and then they learn how to set up and pursue intermediate goals that will bring them closer to that target.)

Commandment VI: Thou Shalt Establish, Review, and Stick to a Monthly Budget. If you and your girl have followed the advice that appears under the First Commandment (above), you've got access to a personal software program that will help you keep track of your checking account. That program will also help you generate a personal monthly budget you can use to estimate future income and expense totals and to evaluate each and every purchasing decision you make. Show her your budget! Talk to her about the tough (and not-so-tough) decisions that you face in finding a way to make it all work. It's easy to complain about how fast the money seems to fly out of your checking account, but it only takes a little discipline to provide yourself with benchmarks that will make it easier for you to decide which purchases fit into your monthly budget and which don't. Make sure both you and your girl have a working idea of what a real, live monthly budget looks like—and the kinds of day-to-day choices that make the allocations a reality.

- Create a budget together. She may have created one with her parents; go over it with her. What does she need on a weekly basis? How much allowance, if any, does she receive? Have her split the money into three piles: long-term savings, short-term savings, and spending money. Does she have what she needs? Where can she cut down? Can she earn more money? If so, how?

Commandment VII: Thou Shalt Secure Appropriate Insurance. What kind of healthcare plan do you have? Explain how it works to your girl and make sure she understands that (at least in our society) medical care doesn't just happen, but must usually be arranged by the families and individuals in need of coverage. Talk to her about what life insurance is, why you have it, and how much you pay for it every year. If you're self-employed and you don't yet have disability insurance, evaluate the policies out there and give your girl your best evaluation of the pros and cons of each. Then cover yourself!

- Help her find out about her coverage. Does she know her policy number? Does she have a card that will help her supply insurance information? What are the steps she would have to take if she had to go to the hospital without her parents?

Commandment VIII: Thou Shalt Know Thy Credit Rating. A great learning experience for both you and your girl is to request your own credit report, and then make your way through the report together. How have purchases and payment patterns been recorded? If you've made mistakes in the past, show your girl that you're motivated enough to find out exactly what they are and that you're willing to find out what you have to do to improve your own credit rating. (Showing your credit report to a Certified Financial Planner, and asking for his or her advice on how best to repair past problems, is one of the best ways to get started.) To find out how to get a copy of your report, you may wish to contact TRW Consumer Credit at 800-682-7654. If you're eager to help your girl build up a good credit history of her own, you may want to encourage her to apply for a department store or student credit card while she's in college. By making a single small purchase, paying off the balance in full, and then canceling the account, she'll be establishing a positive credit record that can be of great benefit to her when she graduates. (See also the cautionary notes on credit card use that appear later in this chapter.)

- Help her cost out the price of something with cash compared to credit payments over the year. Does the item still hold the same value to her? Is it worth the price? Have her evaluate it for herself. Perhaps it's better to save up for the item rather than use credit.

Commandment IX: Thou Shalt Give to Others Who Are Less Fortunate than Thyself. I believe that some form of charitable giving should be part of every mentor's financial plan, and that you should encourage girls to find ways to contribute to causes that are meaningful to them, both through financial gifts and volunteer work. In the previous chapter we talked about gratitude. Gratitude in action means sharing what we have with others. Monetary gifts are one way of offering thanks for the abundance you have been given.

- Can you and your girl offer support—in both cash and hours of your own time—to a local women's shelter? A Girl Scout event? A fundraiser connected to a women's health issue? Find a cause that resonates for both of you and then give whatever you can.

Commandment X: Thou Shalt Acknowledge that Abundance Comes in All Forms. Make sure your girl understands that money is only one aspect of abundance and remembers that gratitude is an essential component of healthy spiritual development. Even though money pressures can seem daunting, it's important to be able to put them in perspective and give thanks for the many gifts in your life, material and otherwise. If your girl sees you doing this on a daily basis, she'll have a model for sane money management in her life, and that's a valuable gift indeed.

- Focus on abundance together. If you haven't already done so, work with your girl to develop a list of ten things she has in abundance; compose a similar list yourself.

All You Need Is Love—and Financial Discipline

"Tough love" in financial matters means helping girls develop long-term abundance and freedom from worries. A marvelous woman known as Sister Betty founded a teen residence for pregnant teen moms in Bushwick, Brooklyn. She was adamant that the girls who stayed with her learn how to budget, balance a checkbook, and save. She sat down and helped them "do the books." She made them put aside money for emergencies and save for their own rent and deposit payment on an apartment. She taught them how to shop appropriately, buying what was needed—not necessarily what was wanted. She was tough, strong and loving.

If you ask Sister Betty to show you pictures of "her girls," she gets misty. Her girls learned how to be financially savvy, and with that they became strong, independent, and fiscally responsible. Thanks to Sister Betty's regimen, they learned how to track their money and make intelligent decisions about where it ought to go.

"I Can't Do This for My Girl! My Own Finances Are a Mess!"

At the risk of repeating myself: No one's saying you have to be the expert here. One of the best things you can do to support your girl's financial future is to appeal for help that will benefit you both. (If you find it difficult to ask for help, read *The Aladdin Factor* by Jack Canfield, Mark Victor Hansen, and Patty Hansen.)

You might choose to schedule a visit to the bank together. Say something like this to the bank manager: "Can you help us both get a fix on what our financial strategies ought to be? We both need help setting up a savings plan—I've got this much income to work with, and my friend here is sitting in so she can see how some of the decisions are made. I've never done this before; I don't know how to do it, but I want to start exerting some control over my own financial situation."

Or say something like this: "You know what? I'm thirty-four, and my friend here is seventeen, and we both need some help on the best way to go about balancing a checkbook.

I'm not up to speed with my home computer yet, and I want us both to learn how to do this. Can you walk us through what we should be doing?"

I know how scary and intimidating the idea of asking for help can be. Many of us were brought up not to talk to people about money, but instead to keep such matters to ourselves. Getting started can be quite difficult.

My sense, though, is that women who are jump-starting their own financial plans can reap a major benefit from the presence of the girl (or girls) in their lives. They can take advantage of two motivating reasons to talk to a professional about the best ways to get started in establishing a personal financial plan: their own future, and the future of the girl whose life they're trying to influence for the better. It's often easier to take the first step when we've got someone else to think of than it would be if we were acting solely on our own. Establishing a mentor relationship can help you "straighten up and fly right" in your own life and follow up on a couple of those New Year's resolutions that have a way of evaporating into nothingness by mid-February.

If mentoring a girl helps you to resurrect a previous commitment to sound financial planning, you and your girl both benefit from that decision. That's good news!

At the most basic level, all you're trying to do is show your girl that there's nothing scary about dealing with money. If you prefer, you can do that by starting out in some very modest ways. Then slowly raise the "degree of difficulty" of your efforts to show your girl how you interact with money.

One great experience is to take your girl out to dinner—and make a point of walking through the final check together, line by line. You pay for the meal, but your girl begins to get a real-world feel for just how much it costs to go out to eat at that type of restaurant.

Painless, right? Now you're ready to move on—together—to some of the more interesting challenges!

Career Development and Growth

The single smartest financial choice a teenage girl can make is probably to avoid having children before she's ready to support them financially or emotionally. Instead, she should commit herself to getting her high school diploma and initiating a period of personal autonomy and independence between the ages of eighteen and twenty-two. If your girl really wants to improve her odds of financial self-sufficiency, she should make a commitment to attend college or lay the groundwork for a career during those years.

For some girls, a state or community college will represent the most realistic opportunity for educational development during this period. For others, working independently in a job that supports career aspirations makes the most sense. Whichever path she chooses to pursue, your girl should get the message from you—loud, clear, and repeatedly—that postponing having children until at least her early twenties, and putting her energy into educational and/or self-sustaining activities during that period, is the best financial course for her.

The facts are stark and undeniable: Girls who drop out of high school experience significantly lower earning potential than girls who get their high school diplomas. Girls who have children during their teen years experience catastrophic, and long-lasting, declines in their earning potential. Your girl may need ongoing help and support in all four of the other support areas—physical, intellectual, emotional, and spiritual—to make finishing high school or earning her equivalency certificate a realistic possibility. And she may need even more intense personal support on all four levels to establish a set of personal values that will help her postpone motherhood until she's ready for it. Your job, as a mentor, is to see that she gets that support and to remind her of the devastating financial and career implications of making poor choices in these areas of her life.

Visit a fast-food outlet. After you pick up your meal, sit down with your girl and ask her whether she wants to be taking orders and passing out french fries ten years from now. When she shakes her head "no," explain that the statistical likelihood of such a career path will increase dramatically if she drops out of school or has a baby while she's still a child herself.

It's never too early to explore exciting work, career, and entrepreneurship choices with your girl. Some of the most innovative work in this area is being done through Joline Godfrey's program, "An Income of Your Own." Ms. Godfrey trains girls to become effective entrepreneurs. Each year the National Association of Women Business Owners (800-266-8762) and An Income of Your Own (800-350-1816) team up to offer scholarships for girls who have developed written business plans. Godfrey runs the training sessions, pairing teen girls with women business owners so that the girls can learn the skills and develop the experience needed to learn how to run a business. She also operates two summer camps for girls who want to start their own businesses.

Another great program that targets pre-adolescents and teens is KidsWay, an entrepreneurial resource program that provides newsletters, business kits for kids, and information for mentors and parents (800-KIDSWAY).

Credit

Our society has made it incredibly easy to obtain credit for the purchases we want to make, but may lack the funds to support today. Unfortunately, it's also incredibly easy for us to charge our way into huge personal credit problems. Young women are certainly not immune from the lures, and dangers, of "no money down" buying.

All too often, young women, especially women living on their own for the first time, see the words "credit card" and conclude that buying just got a whole lot easier. They don't understand the long-term implications of getting in over their heads in debt. All they see is an easy way to get hold of that great pair of shoes they just saw in the window. I should point out, of course, that many adults have precisely the same problem. We're shocked when we finally realize just how much it costs us to purchase merchandise with a credit card.

Your girl needs your help on this score. She needs you to show her that, while credit card purchases are certainly convenient, the card-bearer usually pays a hefty premium for that convenience. It's better for girls to experience that shock early, before they're out on their own and besieged with "guaranteed-approval" card offers—rather than later, when they'll be vulnerable to a serious misunderstanding of the appeals retailers and banks will be sending their way.

Take a few moments to walk through a credit card statement with your girl—perhaps your own! Explain what interest is and what finance charges may accompany a late payment. Walk her through a hypothetical scenario: If you bought a pair of shoes for fifty dollars with a department store credit card, and then took a year or so to pay off your balance, and missed a payment here and there—how much would you actually end up paying for the shoes? It's entirely possible that you may need to change your own credit card spending patterns in order to be an effective mentor for your girl. Here, as elsewhere, there's nothing wrong with learning important lessons together! Share your own fears and concerns with her—she'll begin to understand, on a deep and unforgettable level, the problems associated with excessive credit-card debt.

One of the best ways to support responsible credit-card use is to help your girl put her own tendencies toward impulse spending in perspective *before* she has a credit card. Talk her through impulse purchases—encourage her to use the A-B-C-D model for decision-making that we discussed in the chapter on emotional development. Yes, the outfit she just saw on the rack looks great, and yes, she could buy it right now. But is it the best choice for her? Perhaps she'd benefit from some distance, from a deep breath or two, and from an evaluative review of all the options at her disposal before she makes the decision.

For more information on personal credit issues and effective credit management techniques, contact the International Consumer Credit Association. You can write them at 243 North Lindbergh Boulevard, St. Louis, Missouri 63141.

Negotiation

Sad but true: Men take advantage of women, consciously or not, in many negotiating situations. They use the fact that we may be more likely to avoid conflict and seek reconciliation than they are. Mentors have to embrace the ancient art of haggling, and they have to be willing to use that art in ways their girls will notice.

When I was thirteen or fourteen years old, I was visiting Mexico with my mom and Aunt Lu. I went with them to a bazaar, where I found a suede coat with fringes; I immediately fell in love with it. This coat was a classic of the period—a real early-seventies fashion statement. I was all but salivating for that jacket.

They had enough money to buy it for me—and they had promised to buy me a souvenir of our trip that day. I thought I had it made. My aunt asked the man behind the table how much the coat cost, and he named a price. My mom shook her head and my aunt frowned; they started to walk away, motioning me to follow them.

I was hysterical. How on earth could they deny me that coat? But the more I protested, the stronger their resolve became. After I started to cry, my aunt said, firmly and loudly, for the vendor's benefit, "No, that's it—we're not buying it." And she took me by the arm and led me away from the man's stall.

Once we were a fair distance away from him, my mom and aunt fixed me with a cold stare. My aunt said, "Don't you ever let me catch you showing your emotions when you're negotiating with someone. You've broken the first rule, the most important rule of all in business. You let him know that you want that coat more than anything else in the world. When you're negotiating with someone, you've got to project the notion that whatever you're negotiating over is not that big a deal. If you feel emotions, you've got to hold them in. You have to make them want to sell the coat to you more—much more—than you'd ever possibly want to buy it."

At the time, I didn't much care about all her strategizing. I just wanted my coat, and I told her as much. But my aunt was unrelenting. She said, "You're going to have to learn about bargaining, Pegine. If you're ever going to stand on your own two feet in this world, you're going to have to find a way to keep your emotions in check."

Her point was that anything worth negotiating for was worth strategizing intelligently, and she was absolutely right. But I hadn't grasped that lesson at the time. Without lowering themselves so much as to discuss with me, one way or the other, the coat I had my heart set on, my Aunt Lu and my mom asked me to promise not to launch any more emotional performances as we walked among the stalls looking for my souvenir. I agreed. (What else could I do? She had the money!)

I was heartbroken, but I followed them dutifully as they made their way around the flea market. After about five minutes, we turned a corner that brought us within fifty feet or so of the stall where I'd seen the suede coat. Even though I could tell that the man at the stall was looking my way, I knew better than to stare longingly toward that coat again. I did just what my aunt was doing—I stared straight ahead and kept a sober, uninterested look on my face.

We turned the corner and started walking away again from the man at the stall.

And the moment we turned our backs on him, I heard what had to be the most satisfying sound of the whole vacation. The man was yelling to my Aunt Lu: "*Señora, Señora, está bién, si lo quiere, el precio está bién!*" ("Lady! Lady! Fine! If you want it, your offer is fine!")

I got my suede fringe jacket. Mom ended up paying half of what the vendor had initially asked for. And I learned one of the most valuable lessons of my entire life: Emotion is the enemy of good negotiation. Women owe it to themselves not to let men—or, for that matter, other women—take advantage of emotional responses. We owe it to ourselves not to sell ourselves short. We owe it to ourselves to withdraw from the situation, evaluate, and play the negotiating game to our own benefit. We owe it to ourselves to get the very best terms on a jacket—or a car, or our own salary and benefits package, or a construction bid—that we can find. We owe it to ourselves to learn how to walk away, or at least look, for all the world, as though we're willing to walk away.

If you can find a situation in a flea market, garage sale, or even a contract discussion that allows you to model that behavior for your girl, and then talk about it in terms as memorable and compelling as those my Aunt Lu and Mom used with me on that day in Mexico, you'll be passing along a gift that may well benefit her for years to come.

Don't let others dictate terms to your girl for the rest of her life. Teach your girl the art of putting emotional responses aside during negotiating sessions. Encourage her to establish intelligent, minimally acceptable positions for the negotiation sessions she undertakes—and help her build up the strength to stick to those (unstated) standards by being willing to walk away from the deal when someone tries to take advantage of her. And if you have to practice the art yourself a little before you can model it for her effectively, do so!

Savings

Not long ago I took Mary, one of the girls I'm mentoring, on a visit to a local nursing home. We spent some time with the residents there and helped the staff serve meals and boost morale. The visit was a real eye-opener for Mary. She

learned from talking to the residents that lots of older people are far more financially dependent on their children
than they thought they'd be—a situation that sometimes
leads to intergenerational conflicts and a whole range of difficult family choices. After that experience, the question of
financial management became less of an abstract experience
for Mary. She knew from her own experience that retirement planning was an issue that affected her—and her own
parents, and the family she hoped someday to raise—in a
direct way. In the car on the way home with her, I reminded
Mary that developing a realistic savings and investment plan
was an essential prerequisite to the life she wanted to be able
to live in the future.

As mentors, we have to be willing to ask our girls: What
kind of earning potential do you need to sustain the lifestyle
you deserve, now and in the future? How do you see yourself living ten, fifteen, twenty, or forty years from now?

Or, if that's too scary or remote for your girl right now,
ask her more immediate questions. How does she want to
be living once she graduates from high school or college?
How much money does she want to have saved up by that
point? What are the big-ticket items she'd like to own in
three, four, or five years? How much cash does she want to
be able to spend on a weekly basis?

Once you start hearing some specific answers to questions
like these, you can start asking some new questions: What
needs to happen between now and then to make those goals
happen? Sharing your own (emerging or long-standing)

savings, investment, and retirement strategies, of course, will help.

For both you and your girl, effective financial planning can't take place until you know what your goals are. Remember that different girls have different standards. Maybe your girl hasn't got her eyes set on the opulence of a rock-star lifestyle, but maybe she still hasn't got an idea of the savings she's going to need to amass to make her longed-for trip to Europe a reality. Help her work through what has to happen between point A and point B for outcome C to take place.

You may start by talking with your girl about short-term savings goals, but eventually you'll want to work your way up to a long-range plan for saving and investing. From the time I was about nine years old, my mom had always drummed it into my head that, when I started working, I should save 17% of my salary and put those funds in long-term investments. I didn't listen to her for a long time. Now, as an adult, I've put her rule into practice, and I've been amazed at how fast the money can accumulate if you follow that 17% rule. I have a feeling that I would have put the plan into action more quickly if I'd had a mentor who'd taken a deep interest in the subject with me when I was in my later teen years.

In my case, the only way I could count on saving that money was by having it withdrawn from my checks before I even saw them. I now have my payroll service pull the 17% out before the pay I receive from my own business reaches my hands. That's a strategy that has worked well for me over the years, and I strongly encourage that you consider incorporating it in your own life and sharing it with your girl in discussions of long-term savings plans. Direct deposit works—especially for those of us who know full well that we sometimes lack the discipline to make day-to-day financial decisions that are in our own best interests!

Learn to use direct deposit into a separate account (or a mutual fund) to "pay yourself first"—and encourage your girl to pay herself first when the time comes to do so. Of course, this idea of paying yourself first doesn't mean going on shopping sprees or running up huge credit card bills—instead, it means looking out for your own best interests on a regular basis.

You really are your most important creditor. That means you deserve to set aside a little money for yourself every pay period—preferably the 17% my mother advised. Encourage your girl to take full advantage of her own prime earning years. Help her to develop a long-term savings plan that incorporates the "17% solution."

By the way, I also urge you and your girl to take advantage of the advice in Gordon Williamson's fine book *The 100 Best Mutual Funds You Can Buy* (Adams Media Corporation, updated annually). It's the most accessible introduction to effective mutual fund investing available today.

Planning That Works

Part of planning and saving and budgeting is determining what you're willing to spend on certain things, and then sticking to that plan.

There are all kinds of things we'd love to buy, but we have to prioritize. As I've pointed out elsewhere in this chapter, your girl should learn, from your example, how to deal with impulsive reactions regarding money by withdrawing temporarily from the situation and taking council with herself, just as we discussed in the chapter on emotion.

What are the negative consequences of making a particular purchase choice? What other areas of one's life would such a choice affect? What other alternatives are there? What course of action really makes the most sense from your girl's point of view?

Wherever you can, share stories from your own past about times when you decided you "deserved" something that held immense emotional appeal for you at the time of your purchase—but that carried with it serious drawbacks that you had to come to terms with in the weeks and months that followed. Was it harder than you anticipated to pay back money that you owed? Did you have to pay more in interest or finance charges than you thought you would at the time? Did you have to postpone purchases or commitments that, in the long run, would have meant far more to you than the impulse purchase did? (In other words, did you have to, say, put off a vacation, or put away less money for college expenses than you thought you'd be able to?) Were there feelings of resentment, anger, frustration, or powerlessness that arose as ramifications of one "impulse" purchase—or a series of them?

Share the "downside" aspects of poorly considered financial decisions in as many compelling ways as you can with your girl and encourage her to practice the A–B–C–D technique with you as you shop together and evaluate potential purchases.

Also be sure to share stories that demonstrate how a decision to spend a little extra money for a quality product can make the most sense in the long term. Will a cheap outfit or accessory last for only a month or two before it looks so worn out that you feel uncomfortable wearing it again? It may look flashy on the rack, but that doesn't mean it's the best buy available to your girl. Help her to learn how to buy clothes that serve a variety of different purposes and that look great in combination with each other. Encourage her to buy outfits that will last for a long time and that will look great even when styles shift.★

By showcasing your own methods for making informed financial decisions in both the short and long terms, you help your girl. Even if those decisions are messy, imperfect, frightening, long-delayed, or even, now and then, ill-advised, you'll be showing your girl that grown women do make decisions about their own financial destinies, and that, every once in a while, they learn more than they used to know, and they change their approach as a result.

★ When I visited Spain some years ago, I was amazed at how beautifully the young women there dressed and how few components they needed to make a stunning impression. With just three or four well-crafted elements and a few scarves, they were able to develop some truly exquisite "wardrobes." These young women had a great sense for fashion and value. They invested in just a few simple, well made, fairly expensive dresses or skirts and a few supporting elements, and then mixed and matched their way through the year. American women, young and old, could learn quite a bit by following their example.

That ongoing willingness to tackle the subject, to ask for help when you need it, to go out and dig for better information and act accordingly, is an incredibly important set of skills, one that your girl needs to see in action first-hand.

Don't Make Her Wait

Our public school system teaches its students about mathematics (or at least attempts to teach its students about mathematics, with varying degrees of success). But it doesn't make much of an effort to reach out and help students—particularly female students—understand how important developing a personal financial plan will be for them as adults. Many of the adult women I've spoken to and worked with over the years have expressed deep regrets that no real mechanism existed to help them learn how relatively easy it was for them to set up a simple savings program. They had to figure this out for themselves, and in most cases, they wished they'd figured it out a few years earlier than they actually did. (I know, because I was one of them!)

Don't make your girl wait for five, six, or seven years before she comes to terms with the realities of setting important financial goals and developing workable strategies for achieving them. Show her what you've learned to do—and not to do—and help her accept that even grown-ups find this stuff intimidating from time to time. Even though we may feel some frustration at the task of managing our own money, however, we don't pretend that financial management is a skill we don't need to develop on an ongoing basis, and we don't let our money manage us.

We develop pragmatic plans for living within our means, saving for our future, and establishing investments that make sense for us. By watching us do that, our daughters will learn what our educational system has, thus far, proved unable to teach them; and they'll be in a good position to make sound financial choices that support their own life goals.

9

On Goodbyes

So many of "my girls" have come into my life and then left my life. That's to be expected. I made an impact for a time, and they went on to new experiences.

Sometimes we keep in touch. Sometimes we don't. Almost always, it's clear to me that the experience was a positive one for the girl in question. Always, I try to find a way to be grateful for the opportunity I've had to play a part in any girl's development.

Not long ago, I met the mother of Louisa, a girl I'd mentored some years ago. She had had lots of problems in her relationship with her mother. I had opened my home and my heart to Louisa, listening to her for as long as I could and as respectfully as I could; and then I followed the program you've just read about in order to help her develop physically, intellectually, emotionally, spiritually, and on the level of personal financial management. After a year or so, we said goodbye, and she went to college (a success in itself) and went on with her life. Louisa and I lost track of each other.

When I ran into her mother recently after a seminar I'd given, I was taken by surprise by the strength of the hug I received. Louisa's mother kept saying, "Thank you, thank you, thank you for reaching out to Louisa—she was so difficult as a teenager, but now she and I are working together." As it turned out, the mother owns her own business, and the two former antagonists are now professional colleagues!

Sometimes you hear that kind of story after a goodbye; sometimes you don't. Sometimes your time with the girl simply ends; you're not certain whether or not you made that big a difference in her life, or you feel a sad and quiet place in your heart when you realize you really miss a friend. Sometimes you get to keep in touch with a girl with whom you became quite close. Sometimes a girl simply vanishes from your life, for perfectly good reasons, and there is no goodbye. You never know what happened to her. Always, you try to take what you've learned and apply it to the life of the next girl who needs your help.

There's a saying: "Life is a casting off." It's true for mentors, it's true for mothers, it's true for daughters. I think it's true for all of us. We all move on, move into new stages of development, and try to grow from the experiences in our lives.

For nine years now, my husband David and I have been blessed with a daughter, Andrea. Andrea and I are very close; we still genuinely enjoy being together. Every now and then, she thinks I'm a little too wacky to accompany her in public, but we still value one another's company, and

I rejoice in that. I know that Andrea is growing up now, and like all mothers, I realize that the process is happening much faster than I'd expected (or authorized!).

Andrea is not an adult yet, of course, but she's now on her way to womanhood, just as I was when I was nine. Every day, she's having new experiences and meeting new people. Andrea has entered a new and exciting part of her life, one very different from the period when David and I had the controlling influence over the overall direction of her growth. We are still her parents, and all three of us know that—but we also know that the period of Andrea's "little-girl-hood" is now a fading memory; she's constructing parts of a new, more mature, more discriminating self. We love the person she's becoming—and yet, at the same time, we miss the little girl she once was. That's human. We don't fight that longing or pretend that it doesn't exist. But we don't let it suffocate Andrea, either.

I know full well that my daughter is going to have to deal with situations that I'm not going to be able to guide her through. I also know that I've given her all the love, support, and help I possibly could over the years. Now that she has begun to experience the world through her own eyes and reach out to people in her own way, I have accepted that I can no longer simply scoop her up when it seems to me she's headed for trouble, as I could have when she was a little girl of four, five, or six. The days when her only experiences were those we allowed are long past. Now, for better or for worse, Andrea is experiencing new situations and being influenced by new people. As a mother, and as someone she respects (on good days), I can exert some influence over her path, but I cannot direct it or walk it for her. I must say goodbye to my memory of one Andrea, the younger Andrea—and make room in my heart for the real Andrea, the one who is still growing and changing and adapting in a difficult world that I cannot always control.

As any mother would, I pray for my daughter's safety and I hope that she makes good choices. I need her future mentors—and the women who will affect her future mentors, and the women who will affect the women who will affect her future mentors—to be there for her. A simpler way to say all that is that I need you for my daughter, just as you need me for your daughter.

I need new women to reach out to Andrea and encourage her to immerse herself in the arts. I need new women to introduce her to cultures and traditions she hasn't yet encountered. I need new women to help her discover the wonders of science and experimentation, of nature, of exercise, of sports. I need new women to walk with Andrea down Fifth Avenue at the height of the holiday shopping season. I need new women to show her how to make sense of the next computer program she needs to master. I need new female teachers to enter her life and teach Andrea not only how to spell and use an encyclopedia and write a paper, but also to tell her how they got back up after they'd been knocked down, how they coped with feelings of rejection and confusion and turmoil in their lives. I need new women to tell Andrea how they chose their careers and what inspired them to go into their chosen fields. I need new women to serve as Andrea's professors, her senior colleagues, her bosses—women who will show her how to reach out to others in professional or academic settings. And finally, I need women who will inspire her to pass on the gifts she's received to other girls who remind Andrea of what she was like when she was younger.

No one else will ever be Andrea's mother, but no one else will ever play the role in her life that you can, either. I need all of you to help me with Andrea—to share your knowledge, your wisdom, your insights with her—and the only way I can think of to get you to do that is by summoning my own courage and offering my help in return. If I learn to say goodbye to the "little girl" I've raised (and believe me, it takes an effort on my part); if I celebrate the emerging young woman who now lives with me by encouraging her to connect with you; and if I offer my own commitment to help your girl learn to navigate all the challenging and thrilling experiences of life—then maybe all our daughters will make it through all right.

Recently, a dear friend came over to our house. We started talking about this book; I showed her some of the chapters. She thought back to her own teenage years and recalled the long talks she'd had with her neighbor, a busy professional woman who regularly found a way to take time out of her packed day to talk to my friend and her sister about the challenges of growing up. Now, a quarter of a century later, my friend is the busy professional woman—and the long-neglected memory of her discussions with her mentor had two effects. First, she cried, because she'd never had the chance to say thank you to the woman who'd had such a positive impact on her life. Second, she made a promise to herself, and to me, to reach out to a girl who needed her.

If this book makes you stop and recall your own mentors, feel grateful for the gifts they passed your way, and resolve to help the girls who need you now, then it will have been a success.

Thank you for reading this book. Please write to me, care of the publisher, to tell me of your experiences in using the ideas you've read about. Feel free to share strategies and ideas of your own.

Pegine Echevarria
God bless you!

 *10*

Resources

Who Is Pegine Echevarria, MSW?

Pegine Echevarria, MSW, is a motivational speaker on personal and professional growth for women, girls and Hispanics. Since 1986, she has presented her inspiring, high energy, content-rich keynotes and seminars on career development, leadership and mentoring to large audiences.

She is willing to go to any lengths to inspire, motivate and educate her audiences so that they can be all they can be, do what is necessary, and have the abundance they deserve—in all areas of their lives. She has been a featured speaker for numerous corporations, professional organizations, universities, school districts, government agencies, churches/temples, and women's associations.

Mark Victor Hansen of the *Chicken Soup* series calls her a "Wow of Wows." When Hansen and Jack Canfield were considering whether to publish *Chicken Soup for the Teenage*

Soul, Pegine's enthusiastic plea in favor of it helped convince them to compile it. She was advisor to this best-selling book.

She appears regularly on television addressing issues of teen girls, women and Hispanics. She has appeared numerous times on news shows, *The Montel Williams Show*, MSNBC, *Maury Povich*, *Ricki Lake*, *Rolanda*, and many others. Her high energy makes her a favorite on radio talk shows.

Pegine advocates non-traditional work fields for girls, women and Hispanics, especially in the areas of technology, engineering, and the sciences. Her articles appear in *Workforce Diversity Magazine*, a trade publication for the technology and engineering fields, and other magazines. Pegine is on the board of directors of *blue jean magazine* ®, a leading magazine for girls which celebrates their intelligence and insights.

Pegine has testified in front of congressional members on issues pertaining to women, girls and Hispanics. She was director of a large girl-focused family support center. She ran a women's support program and a family development center for The Salvation Army. She was also top salesperson for a Menswear company and the director of operations for a youth clothing manufacturer. She lived in Spain for several years, where she was director of a nursery school.

Sought as a consultant by leading organizations and companies interested in fostering career development initiatives for youth, women and minorities, Pegine offers curricula that have have won awards for innovative programming.

Pegine received her Masters in Social Work from Adelphi University and her BA from Hunter College in New York.

She also holds a certificate from the Universidad de Madrid and an entrepreneurial certificate from Hofstra University.

For further information to schedule her for a presentation, to find out about her consulting, or to send stories about your mentoring experiences (with girls or at work), please contact:

> PEGCO Seminars for Women, Girls and Hispanics
> P.O. Box 1342
> North Baldwin, NY 11510
> (516) 377-3426
> Fax: (516) 377-4985
> E-mail: Motivationalmentor@msn.com

Here is a list of the very best books, magazines, organizations, and websites for parents and mentors interested in supporting the growth and development of girls.

Books

> *Reviving Ophelia: Saving the Selves of Adolescent Girls*
> Mary Pipher, Ph.D.
> Ballantine Books, 1995

> *Girltalk: All the Stuff Your Sister Never Told You*
> Carol Weston
> HarperPerennial, 1997

> *SchoolGirls: Young Women, Self-Esteem & the Confidence Gap*
> Peggy Orenstein
> Anchor Books, 1995

The Wonder of Boys: What Parents, Mentors and Educators Can Do to Shape Boys into Exceptional Men
Michael Gurian
Putnam, 1997

The Kids' Guide to Money
Steve Otfinoski
Scholastic Books, 1996

No More Frogs to Kiss: 99 Ways to Give Economic Power to Girls
Joline Godfrey
Harper Business, 1995

KidsWay Inc.
5589 Peachtree Road
Chamblee, GA 30341
(888) KidsWay
Fax: (770) 458–1170

Mediations for Women Who Do Too Much
Anne Wilson Shaef
Harper San Francisco, 1996

Designing a Woman's Life: Discovering Your Unique Purpose and Passion
Judith Couchman
Multnomah, 1995

Cybersurfer: The OWL Internet Guide for Kids
Nyla Ahmad
OWL Books, 1996

*The Romance of Risk: Why Teenagers Do The Things
They Do*
Lynn E. Ponton, M.D.
Basic Books, A division of Harper Collins Books, 1997

*Chicken Soup for the Teenage Soul: 101 Stories of Life,
Love & Learning*
Jack Canfield, Mark Victor Hansen, and Kim
Kirberger
Health Communications, Inc., 1997

The Aladdin Factor
Jack Canfield, Mark Victor Hansen, and Patty Hansen
Berkley Books, 1995

*Mentoring: The Most Obvious Yet Overlooked Key to
Achieving More in Life Than You Dreamed Possible:
A Success Guide for Mentors and Protégés*
Floyd Wickman and Terri Sjodin
Irwin Professional Publishing, 1996

Megatrends for Women: From Liberation to Leadership
Patricia Aburdene and John Naisbitt
Fawcett Books, 1993

Great Transitions: Preparing Adolescents for A New Century
Carnegie Corporation of New York, 1995

Teen EmPower: Solid Gold Advice for Those Who Teach, Lead & Guide Today's Teens from American's Top Speakers and Authors in Education
Michael Scott Karpovich, CSP and Jimmy Cabrera, CSP
Patterson Printing, Benton Harbor, Michigan
(800) 718-3367; (800) 437-4226

Dig Your Well Before You're Thirsty: The Only Networking Book You'll Ever Need
Harvey Mackay
Doubleday, 1997

The 100 Best Mutual Funds You Can Buy
Gordon Williamson
Adams Media Corporation, updated annually

Magazines

blue jean magazine ®
Pittsford–Victor Road, Suite 201-203
Victor, NY 4564-9790
(888) 4-blu-jean (888-4-258-5326/7353)

American Girl ® Magazine, (800) 234-1278

Organizations and People

American Association of University Women
1111 Sixteenth Street, NW
Washington, D.C. 20036
(202) 785-7700
Fax: (202) 872-1425
Tdd: (202) 785-7777
E-mail: info@mail.aauw.org

Girls Scouts of the USA
(212) 852-8000 or (800) 223-0624 or contact your
local council

Girls Incorporated National Headquarters
30 East 33rd Street
New York, NY 10016-5394
(212) 689-3700
Fax: (212) 683-1253
E-mail: HN3580@handsnet.org

Girls Incorporated National Resource Center
414 West Michigan Street
Indianapolis, IN 46202-3233
(317) 634-7546
Fax: (317) 634-3024
E-mail: HN3580@handsnet.org

Institute for Women in Trades, Technology & Science
3010 Wisconsin Avenue, NW, Suite E-10
Washington, D.C. 20016-5052
(202) 686-7275
Fax: (202) 686-1291
E-mail: iwitts@aol.com
http://www.serve.com/iwitts

An Income of Your Own
1804 Burbank Blvd.
Burbank, CA 91506
(800) 350-1816

Entrepreneurship Training for Girls

National Association of Women Business Owners
110 Wayne Avenue, Suite 830
Silver Spring, MD 20910
(303) 608-2590
Fax: (301) 608-2596

Take Our Daughters to Work ® Day sponsored by the
Ms. Foundation
120 Wall Street, 33rd floor
New York, NY 10005
(212) 742-2300
Fax: (212) 742-1531
E-mail: todtwcom@ms.foundation.org
http://www.ms.foundation.org

Big Brothers and Big Sisters
230 North 13th Street
Philadelphia, PA 19107
(215) 567-7000

Dare to Dream Foundation
3790 Kings Way
Boca Raton, FL 33434
(561) 883-9918
www.daretodream.org

Ellen Marie, MS
Youth Support, Inc.
3471 West Broadway Avenue #122
Minneapolis, MN 55422
(612) 529-6884 (52-YOUTH)
youthspt@aol.com
Youth Speaker on abstinence and positive choices

Quicken ®
Easy-to-use financial management program
(800) 224-0517

Institute of Certified Financial Planners
(718) 236-7077

TRW Consumer Credit
(800) 682-7654

International Consumer Credit Association
243 North Lindbergh Boulevard
St. Louis, Missouri 63141

Websites for Girls Ages 8-15

Cool Kids Links
http://rowell.pair.com/links.htm

Purplemoon
www.purple-moon.com

American Girl
www.americangirl.com/ag/ag.cgi

A Girls World On-line Clubhouse
www.agirlsworld.com

Girl Tech
www.girltech.com

Websites for Young Women Ages 13-21

blue jean magazine ®
www.bluejeanmag.com

Just for Girls
www.girlscouts.org/girls/

KidsWay Inc.
www.kidsway.com

The Entrepreneurial Development institute
www.bedrock.com/tedi/tedi.htm

Girls Inc.
www.girlsinc.org

Junior Achievement
www.ja.org

Girl Tech
www.girltech.com

Websites for Women

Today's Girls, Tomorrow's Women
www.familycenter.org/girls.htm

American Association of University Women
www.aauw.org/

Action guide for girls education
www.igc.org/beijing/ngo/girls.html

Ms. Foundation for Women
www.sherryart.com/daughters/ms.html

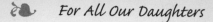

Girl Scouts of the USA
www.gusa.org

Dare to Dream Foundation
www.daretodream.org

KidsWay Inc.
www.kidsway.com

Kidsmoney
www.pages.prodigy.com/kidsmoney

Girl Tech
www.girltech.com